BCIM-ECONOMIC CORRIDOR

The Road Ahead

BCIM-Economic Corridor

The Road Ahead

Editors

Rajiv K. Bhatia
Rahul Mishra

INDIAN COUNCIL OF WORLD AFFAIRS

PENTAGON PRESS

BCIM-Economic Corridor: The Road Ahead

Editors: Rajiv K. Bhatia, Rahul Mishra

ISBN 978-81-8274-843-9

First Published in 2015

The views expressed in this volume are of individual contributors and do not represent the viewpoint of the editors or the Council.

Published by
PENTAGON PRESS
206, Peacock Lane, Shahpur Jat,
New Delhi-110049
Phones: 011-64706243, 26491568
Telefax: 011-26490600
email: rajan@pentagonpress.in
website: www.pentagonpress.in

Branch
Flat No.213, Athena-2,
Clover Acropolis,
Viman Nagar,
Pune-411014
Email: pentagonpresspune@gmail.com

Printed at Aegean Offset Printers, Greater Noida, U.P.

CONTENTS

BCIM-EC: CHALLENGES AND PROSPECTS

Preface

With the aim to deepen our mutual understanding and to contribute to the further evolution of the concept of cooperation amongst the BCIM countries: Bangladesh, China, India and Myanmar, the Indian Council of World Affairs (ICWA) organised a day-long seminar on Bangladesh, China, India and Myanmar-Economic Corridor (BCIM-EC) on December 5, 2013. The seminar was a great success as it was of particular interest to scholars from eastern India. I wish to particularly applaud the work of BCIM veterans who have had to persevere long before they began to be taken seriously. Without their initiatives, stamina and dedication, the discourse on BCIM would not have made a mark.

The ICWA seminar was an intellectual activity with a purpose. In December 2013, India's official delegation was in the midst of preparations for the first meeting of the Joint Study Group, to be held in China in late December 2013. The Joint Study Group meeting involved "discussions on concepts and alignments of the economic corridor" and study of "specific programmes on building the BCIM- EC." The Ministry of External Affairs, Government of India, therefore, requested ICWA to create an opportunity for seeking out and listening to opinions and recommendations of select members of the strategic community, including leading experts from India's North East Region (NER). I welcome the Government's willingness to hear our perspective that could inform the Ministry's brief and, thus, mould policy formulation as well as the eventual design of the BCIM-EC cooperation package. The present volume is an endeavour in this direction.

I am confident that when the history of the BCIM Forum is written, the year 2013 will deserve a very special mention. An exercise that began as the Kunming Initiative in 1999 has today traversed a long path to culminate in the Kolkata-to-Kunming Car Rally in February 2013 and the 11th meeting of the Forum in Dhaka, also in February 2013. This formed the backdrop to the understanding reached between the Governments of China and India, which was also reflected in the Joint Statement issued after the maiden foreign visit of the Chinese Premier Li Keqiang to India in May 2013, and our former Prime Minister Manmohan Singh's visit to China in October 2013. The former Prime Minister's statement referred to an agreement to consult other parties on "establishing a Joint Study Group on strengthening connectivity in the BCIM region for closer economic, trade and people-to-people linkages, and initiating the development of a BCIM Economic Corridor."

Debate on the co-relation between the security and development dimension of our external policy and the role of the NER in India's Look East Policy (LEP) has gone on for long, both within and outside Government. I am convinced that President of India, Pranab Mukherjee's, has spoken the last word on this complex theme. Addressing different audiences in Arunachal Pradesh and Nagaland (on November 29 and December 1, 2013 respectively), he articulated the quintessence of the Indian State's point of view: "'Look East' policy is that India must find its destiny by linking itself more and more with its Asian partners and the rest of the world. India's future and economic interests are best served by closer integration with the rest of Asia."

In his other remarks, during a recent visit to NER, the President underscored the fact that the North East states are key stakeholders in India's LEP and they should "lead in making our neighbours partners in our development and harnessing opportunities emerging from the rise of India and India's growing economic integration with the region." He also stressed the need for the Centre and the states to work together to achieve these goals.

This aptly sets the stage for this edited volume on BCIM. We have tried to avoid using old arguments, empty generalities, and polemics reflecting mutual recrimination. The contributors to this edited volume have paid concentrated attention to spelling out a realistic vision of BCIM-EC by defining its contours, potential scope, integral elements, and practical modalities for realising the vision.

The papers presented during the seminar along with a report on the discussions held are presented to and shared with interested scholars through this publication. We hope it represents a useful addition to the existing knowledge on the subject.

June 25, 2015

Ambassador Rajiv K. Bhatia
Director General, ICWA

List of Contributors

Prof. E Bijoykumar Singh. For the last thirty years, Prof Singh has been studying various aspects of the economy of the NER of India. He was in the core committee for the preparation of Manipur state Development Report and Manipur Human Development Report sponsored by the Planning Commission, Government of India and UNDP respectively. He was in charge of Indo-Myanmar sector in the study on "Expansion of North East India's Trade and Investment with Bangladesh and Myanmar" by Research and Information System for Developing Countries (RIS) in 2010.

Subir Bhaumik is Senior Fellow, CSIRD-Kolkata and senior editor at bdnews24.com. He is a former BBC East India bureau chief and a Queen Elizabeth House fellow at Oxford University. He is author of "Insurgent Crossfire: Northeast India" and "Troubled Periphery: Crisis of India's Northeast". Besides having edited two other books, one on Bangladesh's Chittagong Hill Tracts, Bhaumik has contributed to more than 20 books on Northeast India, Bangladesh, Myanmar and on regional issues. He writes extensively on BCIM countries in the Indian and foreign media.

Prof. I.N. Mukherji is currently Senior Consultant, Research and Information System for Developing Countries, New Delhi. Professor Mukherji, a gold medalist from Patna University, from where he did his Masters (MA) in Economics in 1964. Later in 1966, he did his Master of Science (Msc.) in Economics and Administration from Loughborough University of Technology (UK) under a scholarship from Burmah Shell. During the period 1971-2008 he has been with the Jawaharlal Nehru University (JNU). Professor Mukherji is currently Member Editorial Board (India), South Asia Economic Journal, Ex- Member, Editorial Board, Journal of Himalayan Studies, External Member, UGC Special Assistance Programme, Department of Economics, Kurukshetra University, and in Centre for South and Southeast Asian Studies, Calcutta University. Ever since retiring from Jawaharlal Nehru University in September 2008, Professor Mukherji is Senior Consultant, Research and Information system for Developing Countries, New Delhi.

Subrata Kumar Behera is a Senior Research Analyst at Drewry Shipping Consultants.

Dr. T.T. Haokip is currently a Professor of Political Science in North-Eastern Hill University, Shillong. He completed his MA, M.Phil and PhD from North-Eastern Hill University, Shillong. He teaches Foreign policy, Public Administration and State Politics of Northeast India at North-Eastern Hill University.

Prof. Gurudas Das is Associate Professor, Department of Humanities and Social Sciences National Institute of Technology, Silchar. He is one of the most prominent scholars on India's trade relations with its eastern neighbours. Prof. Das has several publications to his credit.

Ujjwal K Paul is a Faculty Member at Department of Humanities and Social Sciences, NIT Silchar.

Tanuj Mathur is a Faculty Member at Department of Humanities and Social Sciences, NIT Silchar.

Dr. Binoda Kumar Mishra is the Director of Centre for Studies in International Relations and Development (CSIRD). He is a Ph.D. from the School of International Studies, Jawaharlal Nehru University, New Delhi. He is also the Secretary General of a civilian initiative between India and China namely the Kolkata to Kunming (K2K) Forum. His current research focus is India-China relationship in the larger regional context. His research areas include traditional and non-traditional security issues, Indian Foreign Policy, Regional Cooperation, Development Issues and Diaspora Studies.

Ravi Bhoothalingam is the Founder, Manas Advisory, Board member. He has served as the President of The Oberoi Group of Hotels, the Head of Personnel Worldwide with BAT, the Managing Director of VST Industries Ltd, and the Director, ITC Limited. A Physics Hons. from St. Stephen's College, a Masters from Cambridge University in Experimental Psychology and an AMP from Harvard Business School, he is the Founder and Chairman of Manas Advisory, a Consultancy practice focusing on Leadership Coaching and India-China business and cultural relations. In addition to serving on the Board of prominent companies, he is a Fellow of the Royal Geographical Society, London, Visiting Fellow at the Institute of Chinese Studies, Delhi University, and Visiting Professor at the Administrative Staff College of India. He currently serves on the Editorial Board of reputed journals - the China Report and World Affairs. He travels extensively in China, Mongolia, Myanmar, on the Silk Route to China and across Tibet and is actively engaged in the Bangladesh-China-India-Myanmar Regional Development Forum ("the Kunming Initiative") and more recently in the China-India-Nepal Trilateral.

Dr. Rahul Mishra is a Research Fellow at the Indian Council of World Affairs, Sapru House, New Delhi. His areas of interest include politico-military, economic and strategic developments in Southeast Asian countries, regional groupings in Southeast Asia, and Asia-Pacific security issues.

Falguni Rajkumar First direct recruit IAS officer (1972 batch) from the Meitei community of Manipur. Schooling from St. Anthony's High School, Shillong, Degree (Honours) from Hindu College, Delhi in 1968, MA in English Literature in 1970 (University of Delhi) and Msc Transport Economics (Institute of Science and Technology) University of Wales, Cardiff, U.K). He served in the state of Karnataka in the Commerce & Industry department, Transport Commissioner, Chairman and Managing Director of several Public sector undertakings and Addl. Chief Secretary. In the GOI, he worked in the Ministries of Petroleum and Natural Gas, the Ministry of Defence for five years each and as Secretary looking after the North Eastern Council in Shillong from where he retired in 2009. At present he is the Chairman of the Rajiv Gandhi Indian Institute of Management, Shillong. He has authored a book; "THE RAINBOW PEOPLE: Reinventing North East India."

ENHANCING REGIONAL CONNECTIVITY: ROLE OF BCIM-EC

1

BCIM-Economic Corridor: A View from the Corridor

E. Bijoykumar Singh

Introduction

The North Eastern region of India is rich in natural resources, but poverty levels and human development indicators make it one of the country's poorest and least developed regions. The story of the region has been one of the missed opportunities for the Indian leadership over a long period of time. Additionally, institutional mechanisms necessary for inclusive development have been practically negligible. This lack of enough development has led to a sense of alienation, thereby further accentuating the trust deficit amongst the people of the region. As a measure to address the protracted ethnic issues of the region, the local population has been demanding further division of existing state boundaries and territories. One may note that appeasement of such demands has only led to short-term solutions, and has repeatedly raised the bogey of 'Us vs. Others', thus only serving to further aggravate the situation in the region. The potential of the region is yet to be tapped and it is clear that increasing government infrastructure spending and other investment opportunities on the horizon will contribute to an increasingly healthy economy and a growing sense of stability. History is witness to the fact that the partition of India in 1947 adversely affected the trade and commerce and infrastructure in this region developed over centuries, and the problem still persists. On the enormity of change, Goswami writes "The distance between Guwahati and Chittagong is 40 percent of the distance between Guwahati and Kolkata....All exports and imports of Tripura take place through Kolkata port, a distance of nearly 2000 km, though Chittagong port is only 75 km from Tripura."[1] So adverse was the impact of partition that from a thriving region, it, paradoxically in an era of planning, became increasingly dependent and remote from mainland India, and was left with an increasingly stagnant resource base. It is in this context that Upadhyay (2013) sums up the geopolitics of the region: "It was only in independent India that the region became a 'remote corner' surrounded by hostile countries".[2] Hostile environment is a post-independence reality for India.

However, the North Eastern region today is no longer being seen as the periphery of India but as the centre of a thriving and integrated economic space linking two dynamic regions through a network of highways, railways, pipelines and power transmission lines criss-crossing the region. It is in this context that the chapter discusses the importance of BCIM-EC, particularly for the North Eastern region of India.

The Idea of BCIM-Economic Corridor

The idea of BCIM-EC is turning out to be a breakthrough in the development discourse India in general. It seems as if the enthusiasm and hope prevalent at the time of announcement of India's LEP in the early 90s is back again. The initiation of the BCIM-EC gives shape to the vision of a new North East, especially since it has always been considered as the gateway to Southeast and East Asia. Though progress has been slow since the idea of the BCIM was mooted in 1999, there is a feeling, nevertheless, of being at the threshold of big change. A major problem for India is the lack of enough connectivity in the North Eastern region, and the Economic Corridor has immense potential to strengthen connectivity in the BCIM sub-region for closer economic, trade and people-to-people linkages. It holds out great promise for the North East Region since it places the North Eastern states of India at the centre of sub-regional cooperation within the broad parameters of LEP. Rightly, thus, it is seen as an important dimension of LEP. One may argue that with the BCIM, India is endeavouring to bring its North East to the forefront, which in turn will boost India's LEP. As stated in the High Level Commission Report to the Prime Minister published in 1997:[3]

> With the recent softening of geo-political rigidities following understandings with China, then Myanmar and most especially with Bangladesh, the North East is no more a burdensome peripheral region somewhere out there, but is poised once again to resume its dynamic role as a bridge to the booming economies of Southeast Asia and Southwest China to mutual benefit.

BCIM envisages wider market access to some of the fastest growing markets in the region. Trade would, thus, serve as a driver for rapid economic development of the region. However, physical connectivity is needed to reap the benefits of trade opportunities by integrating road, rail, air and water ways in the region, accompanied by Information and Communication Technology (ICT) connectivity. To strengthen connectivity between North Eastern Region (NER), China and Myanmar, the reconstruction of the Stillwell road is already underway. The Stillwell road, built during World War II, connected NER to Myanmar and China. It passed through Ledo, Lekhapani and Pangshu Pass in India, Myitkina and Lashio in Myanmar and Kunming, the capital of Yunnan province, in South West China. Of its 1700 km stretch, 173 km is in India; about 727km in Myanmar and 800 km in China. The reconstruction of the Stillwell road as the Trans-Asian Expressway—together with Trans-Asian Railway—could link Myanmar, South-West Chinese trading centres and the Southeast Asian region.[4] The Stillwell road will shorten the 6000 km trip from the current India-Chinese trade route through the Straits of Malacca to less than one third.

Though the stretch from Myitkina to Kunming is well developed, the stretch from Ledo to Myitkyina needs rebuilding. From Lashio, the North Eastern route to Kunming is well connected by rail and road to the provinces of South and Central Myanmar bordering Laos, Thailand, Malaysia and Singapore. Kunming is connected to Hong Kong by an express highway. Once completed, Indian exports via the Stillwell road could move from the the Eastern-most border of Arunachal Pradesh to Kunming in Yunnan in two days; to Yangon in Myanmar in two and a half days; to Bangkok in Thailand in four days and to Singapore in six days.

The alternative route—Tamu-Kalewa-Kalemyo road (160 km)—could be extended by another 250-300 km to join the Stillwell road at Bhamo in

Myanmar, which is also well connected with Kunming. This could be extended from Manipur by 300 km through Southern Assam to the Bangladesh border. Chittagong port would also be closer to the Kolkata port.[5]

The Government of India's commitment to the vision of North East India's economic integration with the geographically, historically and ethnically close East and Southeast Asian countries has to be firm. However, policy initiatives have, so far, betrayed some ambivalence in India's policy, as summed up by Sarma (2013):

> But India's participation in the Asian highway does not reflect the centrality of North East in its scheme of integration of India with Southeast Asia and beyond. Nor does one see any initiatives on the part of the Government of India to take up the reconstruction of the Stillwell road. On the contrary, the Government of India has shown greater interest in building a 1360 km trilateral highway from Moreh in Manipur to Maesot in Thailand via Bagan in Myanmar taking a more southern route away from the emerging Yunnan-Northern Myanmar-Southeast Asia corridor.[6]

GOI's hesitation in this context can be attributed to the following points:

- Overstress on security /strategic consideration
- Prolonged militancy
- Aggressive economic expansion of China in Southeast Asia
- Spread of illegal drug (production, consumption and illegal trans-border inflows) and HIV
- Traditional reliance on the sea route for trade with Southeast Asian countries.

While India's trade with its North Eastern neighbours witnessed a dramatic rise from 1.7 percent to 8 percent during 1987-88 to 2003-4, the trade through the Manipur-Myanmar route has remained at a mere 0.49 percent of India's trade with Myanmar. In short, despite the rhetoric, India's LEP seems to have bypassed the North East.

Importance of BCIM-EC for the Eastern Neighbours

It is evident that at this point of time, it will take considerable time and effort for India to improve conditions in the North East on its own, and it is in this context that the corridor provides an opportunity for the North East to establish links with Eastern and Southeast Asian markets. There are some traditional and non-traditional challenges for India which it cannot deal with on its own. According to Sarma (2013), the binding constraints on the economy of the region, also popularly known as Five I's, are:

- Initial conditions
- Infrastructure lag
- Insurgency
- Imperfection/distortion in factor and product markets
- Indifferent governance

These constraints have clearly affected regional growth processes.[7] One way to diminish this vicious cycle is by advocating for a big push involving several developmental dimensions. For instance, the Five Year Plans in India have failed to deliver prosperity in the North East Region. In such a situation, the issue of economic viability of the continental route and its competitiveness should be examined afresh in the context of recent political and economic developments in the region.

Bezbaruah & Sarma (2013) argue: [8]

> It is true that little of the expanding India-ASEAN or for that matter the India-China trade—has taken place through the North East India-Myanmar continental route. But as this continental route has not been explored yet, it is difficult to dismiss the route as economically unviable for carrying out any such trade....But the Trans-Asian Railway and Highway projects initiated and pursued by UN-ESCAP, coupled with planned connectivity improvements in North East India-Myanmar region, can in future turn the cost calculation favourable for the continental route.

Thant (2011) points to the possibilities very candidly: [9]

> Nearly all trade between India and China today is by sea. But it is unclear what will happen if and when Beijing and Kunming's development plans materialise and China's southwest, with its new oil and gas pipelines, high speed trains and mass tourism, becomes only a day's drive away from India's Eastern edge...what will the effect of more open borders on India be?

The Trans-Asian Expressway will reduce transportation costs substantially and the reduction in costs can transform the remote NER into an exports corridor. Emphasising the importance of China and Myanmar in LEP, Bezbaruah & Sarma (2013) argued:

> ...To enable North East India to profit from the 'Look East' policy, it will be necessary for the Government of India to engage the immediate Eastern neighbours of Myanmar and China for greater cross-country cooperation and closer economic ties.[10]

There are two bogeys: the Myanmar factor and India-China relationship. Reforms in Myanmar seem irreversible. The India-China relationship has become more stable due to mutual economic interests. The slowdown in China's economy has made China look towards the vast untapped Indian market as an outlet for its products and fiscal reserves. In such a situation, both countries can rise above the issue of Tibet and Arunachal Pradesh. Bezbaruah & Sarma (2013) further added: [11]

> ...It is difficult to foresee India's enhanced economic ties with countries in its Eastern neighbourhood, automatically turning the remote border region of the North East into a gateway to Asian prosperity. But if the planned connectivity improvements materialise and India's unease with its Eastern neighbours like China get sorted out, not only will the North East emerge as India's gateway to the East, but North East India-Myanmar can emerge as a major trade corridor between South Asia on the one hand and East and Southeast Asia on the other.

We, thus, have a huge stake in improving the India-China relationship. How does China look at these developments? Thant has rightly pointed out that "China's nightmare scenario is the involvement of the US or India blocking the Malacca Straits. But India's nightmare is Chinese naval supremacy across the Indian Ocean."[12] He further added that "for China, all roads have led to Burma. The opening up of trade between Yunnan and Burma and the strengthening of ties is seen, more generally, in China as a strategic hedge against over dependence on the Straits of Malacca as well as a way of developing a new outlet to the sea for its landlocked interior."[13]

On the issue of NER, in an article, Bhaumik (2014) discusses in detail the problems plaguing NER, ending with a pessimistic note that in the context of such problems, the proposed continental route traversing across the region would not be able to compete with the maritime route. He further argues that "it will never be easy for India to 'Look East' through its North East, which opens onto the conflict-ridden, poorly developed areas of Myanmar, mostly located on difficult physical terrain."[14] Another view reflects deep apprehension of the possible impact of the Old Silk Road and the New Silk Road on the fragile economies of India's North Eastern states, Bhutan and Nepal.

Summing up the dilemma of the Indian policy makers, Thant (2011) writes: [15]

> A more confident Delhi should allow the North East to become a regional hub, like Yunnan is trying to be. Only this will lead to positive change and real development. But there is a fear of letting go, a fear that greater openness, greater trade with China, a road to China through Burma, will be to China's advantage.

Bhaumik (2014) highlights the usual dilemma of policy makers by arguing that "it makes definite logistic and economic sense to try using the North East to open out to South West China, which, unlike Southeast Asia, is landlocked....This introduces an element of uncertainty on whether or not India is prepared to take some risks that go with allowing the "Look East' to blossom to its full potential by using the North Eastern "land bridge'."[16]

The risk is there, but so is the opportunity. What we need is proper risk management which will alienate stereotype description of the North East. If conditions are created for the region to blossom to its full potential, the stereotype image of the region will also disappear. A developed and peaceful North East is the best way to manage India's interests along the international border. It is in this context that Thant (2011) argues: [17]

> What if peace actually comes to North East India after six decades? The peaceful and democratic North East, with its ethnic and cultural diversity, would be a compelling example for others. China has been unmatched at building new infrastructure and its roads through Burma may well bring an era of Chinese ascendency. But roads go two ways and in a slightly different world, it could well be India or even Burma that influences Yunnan's future, as much as the other way round.

Approaches to Look at LEP

It goes much beyond what we understand to be the core of our LEP. Thant (2011), gives the most inclusive interpretation of the purpose of LEP: [18]

> Here, looking East was not only about economic policy and political strategy, but related as well to issues of identity and fresh connections... Local peoples were not just pawns on a map, but actively shaping the landscape, identifying their own interests and, as in this case, looking beyond their immediate neighbourhoods for ideas about who they were and what they wanted to be.

The possibility of developing North East India as a gateway to South and Southeast Asian countries is no longer a theoretical proposition. There are prospects for increasing investment and productivity, particularly in the export-oriented sectors through greater international participation. Investigation of the grey area between threat perception and the compulsion of interdependence should be given the importance it deserves.

The Policy Options

There is a belief that the NER will not be able to stand up to the competition and exposure, such a corridor is expected to usher in the region, if it is not given the opportunity to grow. That is a vicious cycle. Another debilitating vision is the vision that of industrialisation based on comparative advantage.[19] It is well-known that products in which the region has a comparative advantage do not have a large market in Southeast and East Asia. The creation of comparative advantage in this region to take advantage of such neighbourhood markets has never been seriously debated. In the Lin vs. Chang debate, a strong argument is made by Chang that a country needs to defy its comparative advantage in order to upgrade its industry.[20] Chang argues that:[21]

> ...given the nature of the process of factor accumulation and technological capability, it is simply not possible for a backward economy to accumulate capabilities in new industries without defying comparative advantage and actually entering these industries before it has the 'right' endowment factors.

Establishing industries without any local resource has been successfully tried in many places. Japan produces the finest steel in the world yet iron ore has to be imported. In the North East also, a similar strategy should be tried to initiate the growth process. Policy makers should not go by textbook rules; instead, they should go for unconventional approaches. The objective is to launch the region in a self-sustaining and ever-rising trajectory which calls for a new look at benefits and costs. It is in this context that BCIM-EC is going to play a very important role.

Another industry with immense potential for rejuvenating the region is tourism.[22] The natural wealth and culture of the region can be marketed as is done for any place of tourist interest. What Indonesia's Bali Island, considered one of the most beautiful in the world, has managed to achieve by marketing its beaches and culture may also be realised by the NER by marketing its forests, hills and culture. Bhutan is another example of a tourism-based economy. But this industry has not grown fully in the region due to archaic restrictions on tourist movements and lack of development of tourist 'infrastructure'. Tourism is not a homogenous product and the wants of tourists need not be standardised.

The hydel power resources in the region should be a major driver of change by creating an ambient environment. Generating power and selling it within and outside the region will not be as powerful a driver; on the contrary, adequate electricity should be made available to the industrialisation of the region as a whole through backward and forward linkages, especially since the region is trapped in a vicious cycle of low absorptive capacity and low growth and giving the people money to buy electricity may not be the correct approach. Also, mega hydel projects should have the people's mandate, without which they could get mired in litigation and protests.

Conclusion

The plea is to give the NER an impetus irrespective of costs because a peaceful and prosperous NER is a far better proposition than a troubled NER. The money currently being spent on law and order in the region because of lack of development can be saved since development can take care of destabilising forces. The question now arises—is the NER ready in its new role as a transnational entry point and gateway and if not, how can it be made ready for such a challenge? Skill creation and entrepreneurship training can be partial responses at best.

The region should be allowed to rediscover itself. LEP is an opportunity and BCIM-EC will make it more meaningful. Policy makers should try to understand the type of handholding the region needs and should be prepared to bear some short term costs for long term gains. They should be ready for bold and imaginative initiatives. The people in the region should be trusted to contribute to the nation-building. Once they rediscover themselves as citizens of this great nation, comparative advantage can be reworked.

BCIM-EC is an opportunity for change and it is the responsibility of the people of the nation to ensure that the region does not miss the opportunity. The plea is for encouraging optimum utilisation of resources—including human resources—so that the potential of the region and its people is realised to the fullest extent.

NOTES

1. Homeswor Goswami. "Transport Connectivity and Border Trade of the North Eastern Region" in M. C. Behera (ed.) *North East and Globalisation Issues Betwixt and Between* (Guwahati: DVS Publishers, 2013) pp. 69-77.
2. Vandana Upadhyay. "Looking Beyond the Borders: Globalization and Development of North East India" in M. C. Behera (ed.) *North East and Globalisation Issues Betwixt and between,* (Guwahati: DVS Publishers, 2013) pp. 69-77.
3. Government of India. *Transforming the North East: Tackling backlogs in Basic Minimum Services and Infrastructural Needs* High Level Commission report to the Prime Minister (Delhi, Planning Commission, 1997).
4. Atul Sarma. "The North-East as Gateway to South-East Asia Big Dreams and Home Truths" in M. C. Behera (ed.) *North East and Globalisation Issues Betwixt and between* (Guwahati: DVS Publishers, 2013) pp. 42-43.
5. Ibid., p. 43.
6. Ibid., p. 45.
7. Ibid., p. 50.
8. M.P. Bezbaruah & A. Sarma. "India's Look East Policy: An Opening to Asian prosperity or A False Hope for the North East" in M. C. Behera (ed.) *North East and Globalisation Issues Betwixt and between* (Guwahati: DVS Publishers, 2013) pp. 54-55.
9. Myint-U Thant. *Where China Meets India* (London: Faber and Faber Ltd, 2011) p. 247.
10. M.P. Bezbaruah & A. Sarma. op.cit, p. 62.
11. Ibid., p. 64.
12. Thant, Myint-U, op. cit, p. 268.
13. Ibid., p. 291.
14. Subir Bhaumik. *Look East through North East: Challenges and Prospects for India,* Observer Research Foundation Occasional paper 51 (2014) p.3.
15. Thant, Myint-U, op. cit, p. 291.
16. Subir Bhaumik, op.cit, p.3.
17. Thant, Myint-U, op. cit, p.315.
18. Ibid., p. 311-312.
19. North Eastern Council. *Peace, Progress and Prosperity in the North Eastern Region: Vision 2020,* vol. 1 (2008), p. 26.
20. Justin Lin & Ha Joon Chang. "Should Industrial Policy in Developing Countries Conform to Comparative Advantage or Defy It", *Development Policy Review*, vol. 27, no, 5, (2009), pp. 482-502.
21. Ibid., p 491.
22. North Eastern Council, op.cit, p. 27.

2

BCIM Key to Look-East

Subir Bhaumik

India is involved in a number of regional groupings such as the South Asian Association for Regional Cooperation (SAARC), BCIM and Bay of Bengal Initiative for Multi-Sectoral Technical and Economic Cooperation (BIMSTEC). While it is less than optimistic of achieving much through SAARC because of its apparently insurmountable problems with Pakistan, New Delhi has become ever more interested in sub-regional groupings like BCIM and BIMSTEC to develop trade and connectivity with the Tiger economies of East and Southeast Asia. Though apprehensive of Chinese intentions and weighed down by security concerns and an increasingly adverse trade balance, India is beginning to realise the need to develop closer economic ties with China and keep border tensions and other contentious issues under control. Engaging China is not an option, it is a necessity. China also realises the need to develop closer ties with India, to ensure the latter stays out of any US plan to contain China and to tap its huge market. Hence, Chinese Premier Li Keqiang's attempt to 'handshake across the Himalayas', during his May 2013 visit to India.

In the past two decades, India has pushed ahead with its 'Look East' foreign policy through the relatively under-developed North Eastern states. The Look East via the North East Region hopes to bring much-needed economic development to the troubled region by integrating it with neighbouring economies. This marks a shift in Indian policy, and security concerns that influenced thinking to keep the North East isolated and off-limits to outsiders seem to have given way to a policy of enhancing better connectivity through the region with neighbouring countries. It is now realised that regional groupings that help bring India closer to its Eastern neighbourhood will help boost the economy of the North East region also, which in turn can help stem the problem of insurgency and trade in contraband that leaves the state poorer in every way.

This paper makes four key arguments: (a) if India feels its LEP has to succeed, it will have to enhance greater connectivity between its North East and China's border regions to exploit opportunities provided by the region's biggest economy; (b) if that be so, India will have to strongly follow up on developing the BCIM idea and take it to its logical culmination for it to make sense of its LEP; (c) it will not help to merely promote BIMSTEC, because this grouping is more of a Bay of Bengal initiative and will focus on sea routes rather than land routes through North East; (d) if India is seeking to promote influence in its immediate neighbourhood, it would be much easier to do so through multilateral initiatives like BCIM rather than bilaterally, because in countries like Bangladesh and Myanmar, India risks being seen as a Big Brother on its own.

The paper argues that it makes more sense for Indian industry to look to enhancing trade with Southeast Asia through sea and not land routes because of lesser distances, reduced transport costs and fewer problem of movement. Looking East by land through the North East only makes sense if India tries to access South-West China and use it as a gateway to the huge Chinese market away from the Eastern coast.

India will have to try to use the North East as a land bridge to Southeast Asia more for ending the isolation of this frontier region and boost growth. However, Indian industry will largely have to 'look East' via sea routes to Southeast Asia for trade and human movement for a wide variety of reasons. It makes logistic and economic sense to try using the North East Region to open out to South-West China, which unlike Southeast Asia, is landlocked, but decision-making in India is still divided on issues like reopening the World War II-vintage Stillwell Road or even pressing ahead with the BCIM Friendship Highway (broadly the route taken by the BCIM car rally in February-March 2013). That introduces an element of uncertainty on whether India is prepared to take risks that go with allowing the Look East Policy to blossom to its full potential by using the North Eastern 'land bridge'. Security concerns—especially related to Chinese military presence and

China's growing influence in Myanmar—tend to hold back India in going ahead with initiatives that can allow the 'Look East' policy to deliver the desired results.

It obviously makes much more sense to access Southeast Asia by sea for trade and movement of people than through the North East, for reasons elaborated below:

(a) India's major industrial centres are on the Western and Eastern seacoast, far West, up North or down South from where shipping goods to Southeast Asia by sea makes much more commercial and logistic sense than to move them inland to North Eastern India, with all its accompanying transport bottlenecks. Even export of raw materials like iron ore is easier and cheaper if they are moved through India's Eastern ports like Paradip, Vizag or Haldia from central India for export to Southeast Asia. Moving them inland into North East India and then through trans-regional highways into Myanmar on their way to countries like Thailand will be much more expensive than moving the cargo by sea.

(b) India's major markets and the bulk of its population is in the mainland states and it makes much more sense to bring in goods from Southeast Asia by sea to the ports on the Eastern coast like Kolkata/Haldia, Paradip, Vizag and Chennai. Such imports will be much more cost-effective and time-saving than if they were to be brought in through the Myanmar-North East India land route.

For example, Kolkata is just 1614 kms or 1003 miles (872 nautical miles) by sea from Bangkok. But if some traders want to send a consignment from an industrial location or a mining area in Eastern India to Thailand, it would make much more sense moving the cargo a few hundred kilometres to Kolkata port by road or rail and then by sea, rather than by doing it via the land route. From Kolkata to Siliguri via the "Chicken Neck" is about 600 km, from Siliguri to Moreh on Manipur-Myanmar border is 1022 km and then from Moreh to Mae Sot on Myanmar-Thailand border is another 1360 km—as and when the Trilateral Highway is ready for use. From Mae Sot to Bangkok or anywhere else in Thailand would be another few hundred to nearly 1000 km. The land distance is more than double than that by sea, and calculating relative transport cost, with rising fuel prices, the cost differential between the land and sea route would be enormous.

(c) India's 'Look East' Policy will never work unless Bangladesh facilitates the necessary transit linkages to help India connect its mainland to the North East. Unless the pre-partition transport linkages are re-established and India is able to integrate its road and rail infrastructure with Bangladesh, the North East cannot be easily accessed, and if that is not possible, there is no point for India in attempting to connect to Southeast Asia through the NER. The reality is that India first needs Bangladesh to help access its own North East before using the region to connect to Southeast Asia. So it is important for the success of the LEP to push ahead with the BCIM process because that involves both Bangladesh and Myanmar which are so important to developing India's overland connectivity to China and Southeast Asia.

Bangladesh will allow India greater access to its North East only if it is able to gain major concessions on a host of issues like getting a fair share of the waters of common rivers, major trade concessions that will help it address its highly adverse trade balance with India and solution to its land boundary and maritime boundary disputes with India in a way that Bangladesh can avoid being 'sea-locked'. Again, India-Bangladesh relations so far have tended to be affected by regime changes in Dhaka that introduces a huge element of uncertainty in bilateral relations. India can hope for favourable concessions if Sheikh Hasina's Awami League is in power, but a return to power by the Bangladesh Nationalist Party (BNP)-Jamaat-e-Islami alliance would make things difficult. India had to give up on a gas pipeline through Bangladesh to bring gas from Myanmar's Rakhine state because the BNP-Jamaat Government stymied it when it was in power in 2001-2006.

(d) Myanmar is the only country in Southeast Asia with which India's North East shares a land border. Therefore, India's LEP through NER will largely depend on how India's relations with Myanmar and the internal situation in that country shape up. There is a standard foreign policy argument here that how can India's relations with so many countries of Southeast Asia depend on its relations with one country? Myanmar is passing through an uncertain process of change from military rule to democracy, but it is still grappling with its multiple internal turmoils, some of which—like the one in the Northern state of Kachin—have aggravated in the last two years.

(e) India's success in handling the ethno-nationalist movements in its own NER has been limited. The most important and oldest among them—the Naga movement for self-determination—is far from resolved, despite sixteen years of negotiations. The strong separatist groups in Manipur, from where India is trying to develop its road and rail network into Southeast Asia through Myanmar, are still active and far from neutralised, despite substantial presence of armed forces in the state. Only the two Southernmost states in the region—Tripura and Mizoram—have managed to largely control ethno-nationalist conflict, but Tripura has no border with Myanmar and Mizoram opens into Myanmar's Chin Hills, which itself is a poorly developed and conflict-prone region with abysmal transport and administrative infrastructure. A detailed analysis can highlight the difficulties such conflicts can create for developing modern transport infrastructure to facilitate trade and people's movement with neighbouring countries.

(f) Important decision-making sections within India have great reservation about using the North East to open out to South-West China. Using the 'land bridge' of North East India to access South-West China (and through it other areas of China far away from its Eastern coast) makes much more business sense than trying to access Southeast Asia by land. So 'Looking East' through North East India could work better for India-China bilateral trade if a substantial part of it passes through the region. For example, Shanghai from Kolkata is 4665 nautical miles by sea whereas Kunming from Kolkata (by the route used for the February-March 2013 BCIM car rally) is 3026 kilometres. If one were to add the cost of transport by land over 1500-2000 km from Shanghai to Western or South-Western China, the cost differential is obvious and huge, and that in itself would justify exploring the land route through North East India and Upper Myanmar.

However, military officials in India feel opening the World War II-vintage Stillwell Road to regular traffic will provide China with a great strategic advantage in the event of a war on the land borders of the two nations (as in 1962). Trade officials say the Stillwell road could also be used by China to dump its goods in North East India and, through it, across the rest of the country. The fear of losing a trade war or a conventional war seems to create reverse pressures within India on pursuing LEP to its logical conclusion. There is another much shorter and direct land route to Yunnan through Kibhitu in Arunachal Pradesh, and some have suggested India and China should develop this route rather than the Stillwell Road through Northern Myanmar, which is afflicted by ethnic insurgency and conflict.

One, however, needs to consider the overall changes in the global scenario in which India needs to carefully balance the US and China to further its own interests in Asia. In this, India does not appear to be too comfortable with the growing tensions in Asia that follow US attempts at 'rebalancing' the Chinese assertion of influence in maritime regions contested by its neighbours. The discomfort comes through loud and clear in a speech by the former Indian Prime Minister, Manmohan Singh. Quoting him for record would be useful to understand the anxiety of the former Prime Minister.[1]

> ...If you survey the global strategic environment over the past decade, it would not escape your notice that, just as the economic pendulum is shifting inexorably from West to East, so is the strategic focus, as exemplified by the increasing contestation in the seas to our East and the related "pivot" or "rebalancing" by the US in this area. This, to my mind, is a development fraught with uncertainty. We do not yet know whether these economic and strategic transitions will be peaceful, but that is the challenge this audience must grapple with institutionally.

Manmohan Singh also dwells on the global scenario of 'intense competition':[2]

> While globalisation has induced growing and complex inter-dependencies amongst states and multinationals on the economic and trade front, it has also nurtured intense competition and rivalries in the security domain. Managing this contradictory tenor, which has been highlighted by the global surveillance operation mounted by the US National Security Agency, is also a policy imperative for us. Naturally, our objective must be to acquire tangible national capacity, or what the lexicon now refers to as comprehensive national power.

India's discomfort with the Edward Snowden-revealed US global snooping operation, in which India was an important target, also comes through clearly. India has made its displeasure clear at US plans for drastic troop withdrawals from Afghanistan because it promises a more intense *jihadi* campaign, with the India's Kashmir as the prime focus. Indian and US diplomats have already been involved in some bitter media sparring in Bangladesh, with Delhi backing the Awami League and the US, at least its local envoy, indicating a clear preference for the BNP-Jamaat-e-Islami combine.

After the India-US-Japan trilateral in Tokyo, it is beginning to emerge that Delhi insists on being left to its own 'balancing' in Asia to develop better relations with both China and its neighbours at the same time. Earlier this year, India's former envoy to the US (and former Foreign Secretary) Nirupama Rao tried to drive home this point to an American audience: [3]

> We are part of the Asia-Pacific and an Indian Ocean world that traditionally lived in peace, pursuing the traffic of ideas, the peaceful absorption of different religions without proselytisation, pursuing trade and commerce in a non-polarised, peaceful, common economic space. In our view, more than geopolitical, or geo-economic, this was a geo-civilisational paradigm, a creative space with revolving doors where civilisations coalesced and did not clash. One has only to visit the caves of Ajanta in western India or see the murals of Dunhuang in China's West to see this vision of unity that marked our past. This is the region where we hear the muffled footsteps of historical travellers and thinkers like Boddhidharma of India and Xuan Zang of China beat in our blood, to use a phrase from Rabindranath Tagore. These were lives mortgaged to pilgrimage and voyages of intellectual discovery. We see that past as a rough guide to our future.

Seeing this past as the 'rough guide to our future' may not exactly impress the US. A "geo-civilisational paradigm' is much too woolly a concept for contemporary diplomacy in a country that understands and promotes 'containment' and 'balance of power', key concepts of European colonial-era diplomacy which were given greater relevance and thrust by US policy during the Cold War and after. But India, with its long tradition of non-alignment rooted in a philosophical conviction that 'truth is neither here or there but often in between", has good reasons to attempt to write a new text of diplomacy in what appears to be an emerging Asian century.

So, Nirupama Rao had to remind her American audience at the 'Brown India initiative': [4]

> Guided by the strong economic rationale of our "Look East" policy, Association of Southeast Asian Nations (ASEAN) and East Asian countries, including Japan, China and South Korea, have emerged as

> large trading and investment partners of India. The richness of this engagement is visible in wide-ranging cooperation in areas as diverse as science and technology, tourism, human resource development, transport and infrastructure, health and pharmaceuticals. Indeed, the strategic footprint of our relations with China and Japan, particularly, will exert a major impact on the future of the region.

So, if the core focus of the US 'rebalancing' is to contain China's growing influence by developing an Asian equivalent of NATO, India's 'rebalancing' involves developing balanced relations with both China and its Asian neighbours like Japan, Vietnam, South Korea and other ASEAN countries (as well as Australia) in areas of both trade and commerce and security. That explains why India will do everything possible to avert a conflict-like situation with China that was developing over the Depsang bulge and within six months, pull off the Border Defence Cooperation Agreement (BDCA) with China. That explains why India will agree to take forward the BCIM-EC plan, and why its foreign ministry has started backing the Kunming-Kolkata (K2K) Forum. And that also explains why within a month of Manmohan Singh's Beijing visit, India hosted the general secretary of the Vietnam Communist Party and then plan for similar visits by Prime Ministers from Japan and Australia.

Otherwise, how would one be able to explain India resuming military links with China through joint counter-terrorism exercises in Yunnan, even when Delhi agrees to supply military hardware to Vietnam? The whole idea is to augment national military power but use it only as a last resort option, to avoid any deployment or military exercise perceived as hostile by China.

It is interesting that the Chinese have also reciprocated the US 'rebalancing' (essentially redeployment of the US military especially naval assets to Asia) by some aggressive 'charm diplomacy' in Southeast Asia. Around the same time it was trying to build bridges with India and preparing to host Manmohan Singh in Beijing, Chinese President, Xi Jinping and Premier, Li were touring a host of Southeast Asian countries. Li's proposed 2+7 cooperation framework between China and ASEAN is seen as a game-changer, because it seeks to upgrade the China-ASEAN region into a Free Trade Area (FTA) that will ultimately draw in India and create an integrated market for an area with half the world's population.

During Asia-Pacific Economic Cooperation's (APEC) finance ministers meeting at Bali, China proposed multilateral foreign-exchange swaps with

ASEAN countries to help them face 'external shocks'. This, after having already done similar deals involving 1.4 trillion Yuan in Indonesia, President Xi proposed an Asian Infrastructure Investment Bank to help finance connectivity and crucial regional infrastructure projects like the high-speed railway connecting China to Thailand and Singapore.

China has been countering Washington's efforts to develop the Trans-Pacific Partnership (TPP) with its own heightened negotiations on Regional Comprehensive Economic Partnership (RCEP), an initiative to incorporate existing free-trade zones between ASEAN and other countries. The Yunnan-based "Link Times" was quick to point out:

> Although the US and Japan have tried to highlight the potential military threat posed by China's rise, economic issues remained the primary concern of Asian countries ... for example when the US Government shut down and the threat of a treasury default loomed, it was Japan, US' closest ally in Asia, who joined China in pressuring the US to avoid a default.[5]

Interestingly, this 'Link Times' article talks of Japan and Vietnam as US allies, not India. Both India and China are keen to promote ever greater regional cooperation in Southeast and East Asia to create a 'larger cake" (a Chinese expression for a win-win situation for all). Without this new diplomatic ethos that focuses on cooperation and not conflict or containment, an Asian century will remain a dream on paper, manipulated by non-Asians who would like contests and confrontation to push their armaments exports to a prosperous Asia, rather than allowing it to emerge as the globe's economic powerhouse.

To conclude, one may argue that India has good reasons to take forward the BCIM process with China, Bangladesh and Myanmar. That will help India create a basis for a strong future trans-regional linkage into Eastern and Southeast Asia. It will also help India open up its North East via Bangladesh. It would be so much more difficult for India to send goods into North East from the mainland through a corridor that Delhi might like to develop for this purpose because of reactions in Bangladesh. But if the BCIM land corridor from Kolkata to Kunming works out through Bangladesh, it becomes easy for trade from India to move through Bangladesh to the North East without obstruction. And then, when the land corridor is converted into an economic corridor, it makes things still easier. Bangladesh is already taking great interest in the BCIM corridor, and that should make it easier for India to attain its targets on connectivity in the North East and to the neighbourhood through it.[6]

At the moment, both India and China are less than clear on how to develop the BCIM Economic Corridor, which is why they have agreed on 'joint research' to identify ways and means to go forward. India needs to not rush ahead but slowly explore, and without undue apprehension, a way forward.

NOTES

1. "Excerpts of address by the PM at the Combined Commanders' Conference", *Press Information Bureau,* November 22, 2013, http://pib.nic.in/newsite/PrintRelease.aspx?relid=100796.
2. Ibid.
3. Nirupama Rao. "America's Asia Pivot: The View from India", *Brown University Lecture,* February 4, 2013, http://brown.edu/initiatives/india/sites/brown.edu.initiatives.india/files/uploads/NirupamaRao-America's'AsianPivot'TheViewfromIndia-Brown-IndiaInitiativeSeminar2.4.2013.pdf.
4. Ibid.
5. Sun Xingjie. "Playing Smarter: New Strategic Thinking", *Link Times,* vol.36, November 2013.
6. Dan Steinbeck. "Bangladesh plays key role in China's rebalancing in Southeast Asia", *South China Morning Post,* November 4, 2013, http://www.scmp.com/comment/insight-opinion/article/1345375/bangladesh-plays-key-role-chinas-rebalancing-southeast-asia.

TRADE AND INVESTMENT POTENTIAL OF BCIM-EC

3

INDIA'S TRADE AND INVESTMENT WITH BCIM COUNTRIES

Indra Nath Mukherji and Subrata Kumar Behera

Background

A Joint statement issued at the Eleventh BCIM Forum held in Dhaka on February 23-24, 2013, underscored the need for stimulating and promoting both intra-regional and extra-regional trade and investment in the context of BCIM cooperation. The forum observed that formidable challenges remained in the region in the form of tariff and non-tariff barriers, weak trade facilitation measures, lack of customs harmonisation and obstacles to cross border movement of goods arising from weak infrastructure at—and beyond—the borders. The statement further suggested that greater market access, particularly to low income members of BCIM, could stimulate trade flows within the region. The idea of Regional Trading Arrangement with enhanced preferential market access and supportive trade related investment measures and incentives for particular countries could be considered in this context.

Trade Flows among BCIM Countries

Bangladesh

We first examine Bangladesh's trade with China and India. The period for analysis is from 2006-2012.[1] The data source is the United Nations (UN)

Commodity Trade Statistics (Comtrade) as available with the World Bank; the World Bank Integrated Solution (WITS) database.[2] Bangladesh has not reported data (except for one/two years). Hence, partner country data ("mirror data") has been obtained.[3]

Figure One shows Bangladesh's trade with China. One may observe that Bangladesh's trade with China increased from US$ 32 billion in 2006 to US$ 85 billion in 2012. Its trade with China in relation to its world trade increased from 12.32 percent in 2006 to 14.72 percent in 2012. Its export share increased from less than one percent in 2006 to less than two percent in 2012. Its import share was much higher, increasing from 23.24 percent in 2006 to 26.40 percent in 2012.

Bangladesh's trade with India was much more modest, as will be seen in Figure Two. Its trade value with India increased from US$ 1.89 billion in 2006 to US$ 5.50 billion in 2012. Similar to its trade with China, Bangladesh's trade share with India also increased from 7.31 percent in 2006 to 9.59 percent in 2012. Again, as in the case with China, its export share was miniscule as compared to its import share. During this period, while its import share increased from 1.78 percent to 2.08 percent, its import share increased from 12.54 percent to 16.35 percent. Thus, Bangladesh had increasing trade deficit with both China and India.

China

Figure Three illustrates China's trade with Bangladesh, India and Myanmar (BIM) as a group. As shown in the figure three, China's trade with this group of countries increased from US$ 30 billion in 2006 to US$ 82 billion in 2012. As a percent of world trade, China's trade with this group of countries was quite modest, increasing from 1.68 percent in 2006 to 2.12 percent in 2012. A modest dip in the trade share was seen in the year 2001-2002.

India

As compared to China, India's trade value with Bangladesh, China and Myanmar (BCM) countries was modest, having increased from US$ 7 billion in 2006 to US$ 36 billion in 2012. India's trade share with this group of countries increased from 8.75 percent in 2006 to 9.79 percent in 2012. India's import share increased from 9.30 percent to 11.46 percent, while its export shares decreased from 7.94 percent to 6.97 percent.

Figure One: Bangladesh's Trade with China

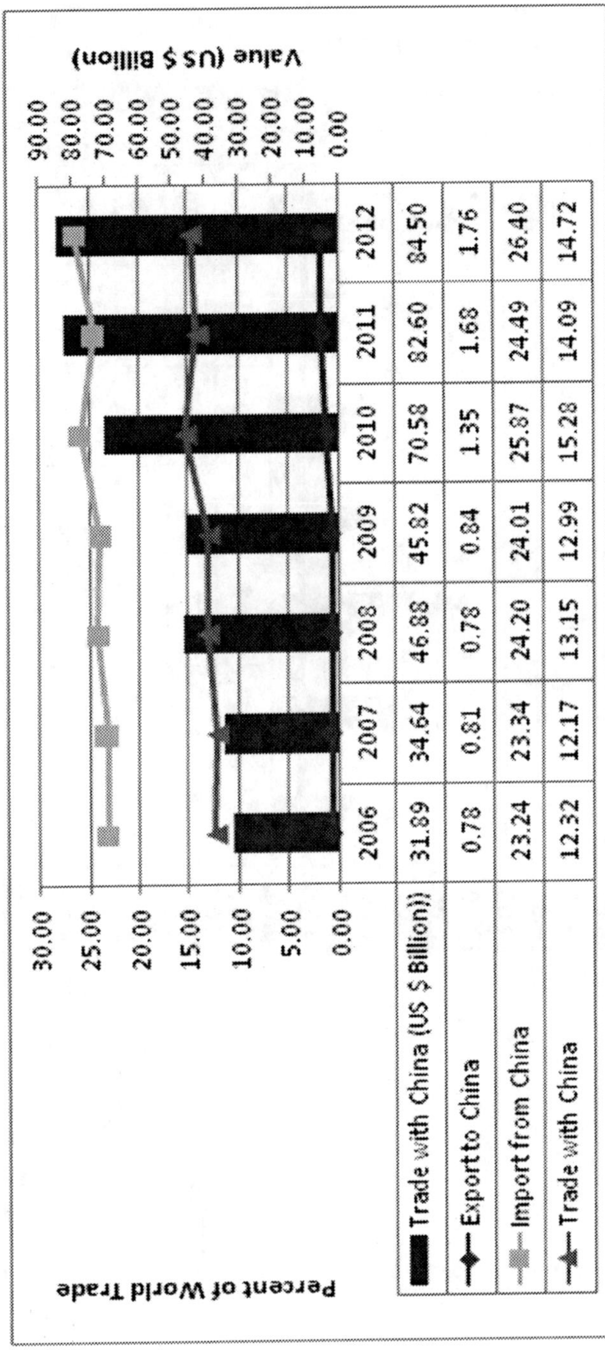

	2006	2007	2008	2009	2010	2011	2012
Trade with China (US $ Billion)	31.89	34.64	46.88	45.82	70.58	82.60	84.50
Export to China	0.78	0.81	0.78	0.84	1.35	1.68	1.76
Import from China	23.24	23.34	24.20	24.01	25.87	24.49	26.40
Trade with China	12.32	12.17	13.15	12.99	15.28	14.09	14.72

Source: Authors' estimate based on World Bank data, World Integrated Trade Solution (WITS) database.

Figure Two: Bangladesh's Trade with India

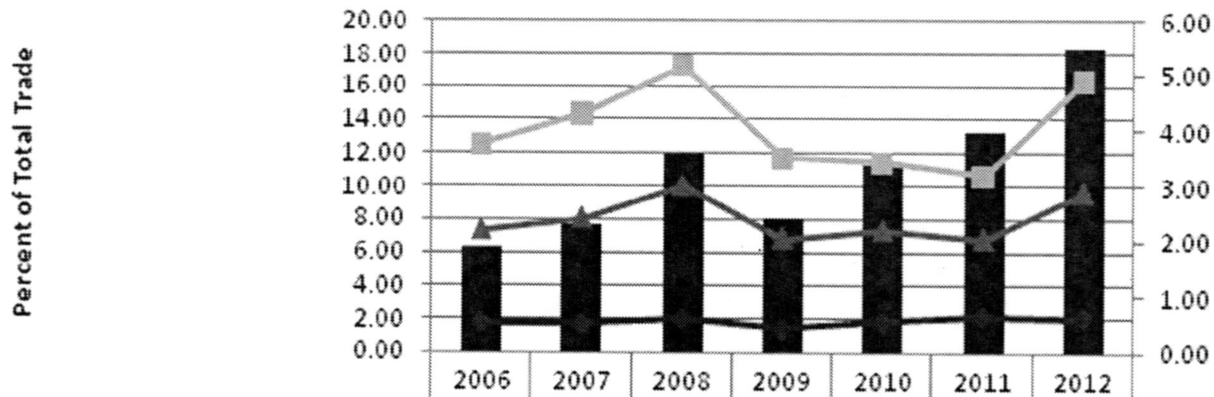

	2006	2007	2008	2009	2010	2011	2012
Trade with India (US $ Billion)	1.89	2.30	3.57	2.41	3.37	3.98	5.50
Export to India	1.78	1.65	1.96	1.40	1.79	2.16	2.08
Import from India	12.54	14.38	17.23	11.77	11.50	10.68	16.35
Trade with India	7.31	8.07	10.02	6.84	7.31	6.80	9.59

Source: Authors' estimate based on World Bank data, World Integrated Trade Solution (WITS) database.

Figure Three: China's Trade with BIM Countries

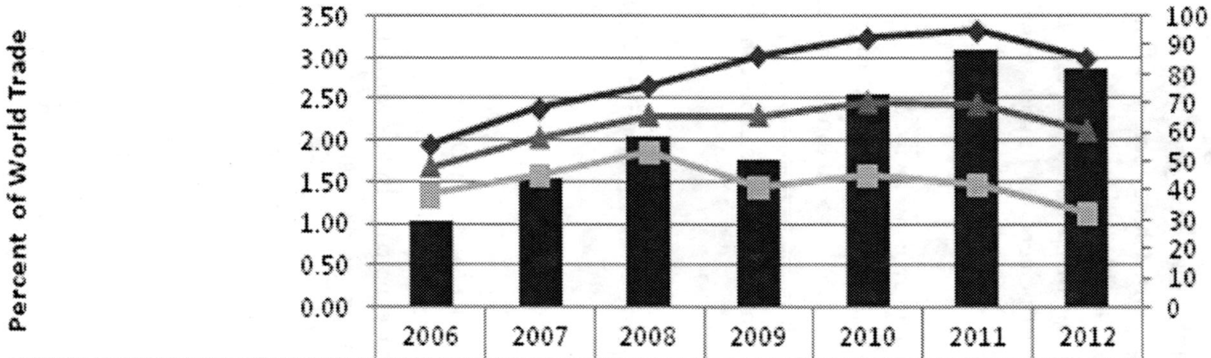

	2006	2007	2008	2009	2010	2011	2012
China's Trade (Right Axis)	30	44	59	51	73	89	82
China's Exports	1.95	2.39	2.66	3.03	3.24	3.33	2.99
China's Imports	1.34	1.58	1.86	1.44	1.58	1.46	1.13
China's Trade	1.68	2.03	2.31	2.30	2.46	2.43	2.12

Source: Authors' estimate based on World Bank data, World Integrated Trade Solution (WITS) database.

Myanmar

Due to lack of reported data, as in the case of Bangladesh, we take "mirror" data from Myanmar's partner countries in the region. It will be observed in Figure Five that Myanmar's trade with China increased from US$ 1.46 billion in 2006 to US$ 6.97 billion in 2012. Its trade share increased from 17.96 percent to 29.65 percent during this period. Its export share increased sharply from 5.45 percent to 15.79 percent. Its import share was higher, but it increased more modestly from 34.56 percent to 37.12 percent during the same period.

Myanmar's trade with India is illustrated in Figure Six. Myanmar's trade value with India was considerably modest as compared to its trade with China. Its trade value increased from US$ 0.83 billion in 2006 to US$ 1.87 billion in 2012. Its trade share with India declined from 10.17 percent to 7.97 percent. During this period, while Myanmar's export share with India increased, its import share declined.

Additional Market Access Potential of India with BCIM Countries

All Matched Products

In this section, we examine Additional Market Access Frontier (AMAF) of India with the rest of BCIM countries. In order to evaluate AMAF of India with other BCIM countries, we have matched India's world imports of say, product 1 with the partner countries' world imports and then deducted the existing exports to the partner country to arrive at India's AMAF with its partner. We have then reversed the relationship to estimate how much AMAF India's partner country has with India. When the AMAF for each matching product is summed up, we get the total AMAF that a supplying country has with its partner. The details of the estimate have been presented in Technical Appendix 1.

Table Seven summarises the AMAF of India with its partners in the BCIM region and the same of the partner countries with India.

Figure Four: India's Trade with BCM Countries

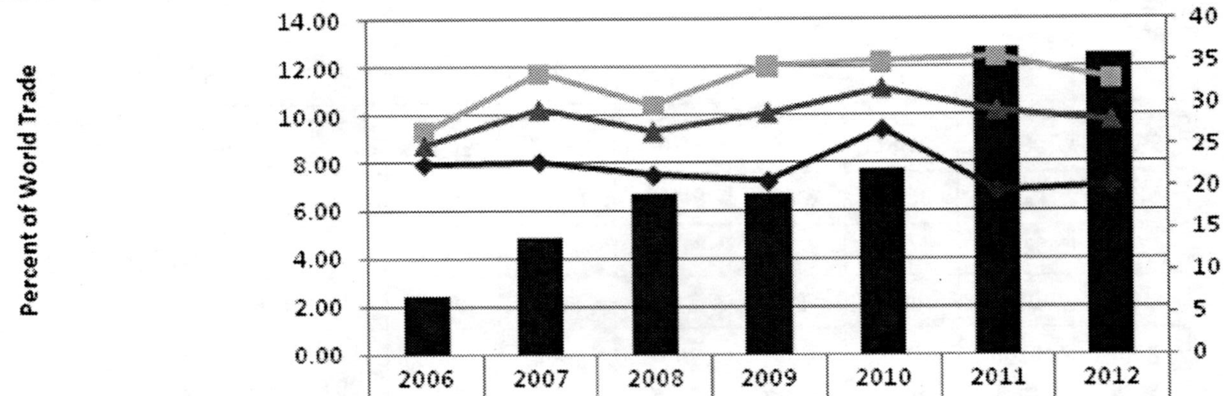

	2006	2007	2008	2009	2010	2011	2012
India's Trade (Right Axis)	7	14	19	19	22	37	36
India's Exports	7.94	8.03	7.46	7.22	9.40	6.83	6.97
India's Imports	9.30	11.72	10.40	12.02	12.21	12.40	11.46
India's Trade	8.75	10.24	9.32	10.11	11.12	10.20	9.79

Source: Authors' estimate based on World Bank data, World Integrated Trade Solution (WITS) database.

Figure Five: Myanmar's Trade with China

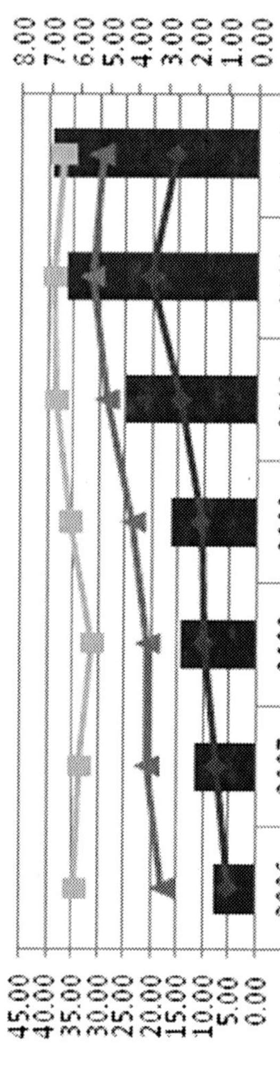

	2006	2007	2008	2009	2010	2011	2012
Trade with China (Right Axis)	1.46	2.08	2.63	2.91	4.44	6.50	6.97
Exportto China	5.45	7.66	10.12	10.77	14.77	20.28	15.79
Import from China	34.56	33.81	31.46	35.49	38.38	38.74	37.12
Trade with China	17.96	20.85	20.69	23.50	28.48	31.37	29.65

Source: Authors' estimate based on World Bank data, World Integrated Trade Solution (WITS) database.

Figure Six: Myanmar's Trade with India

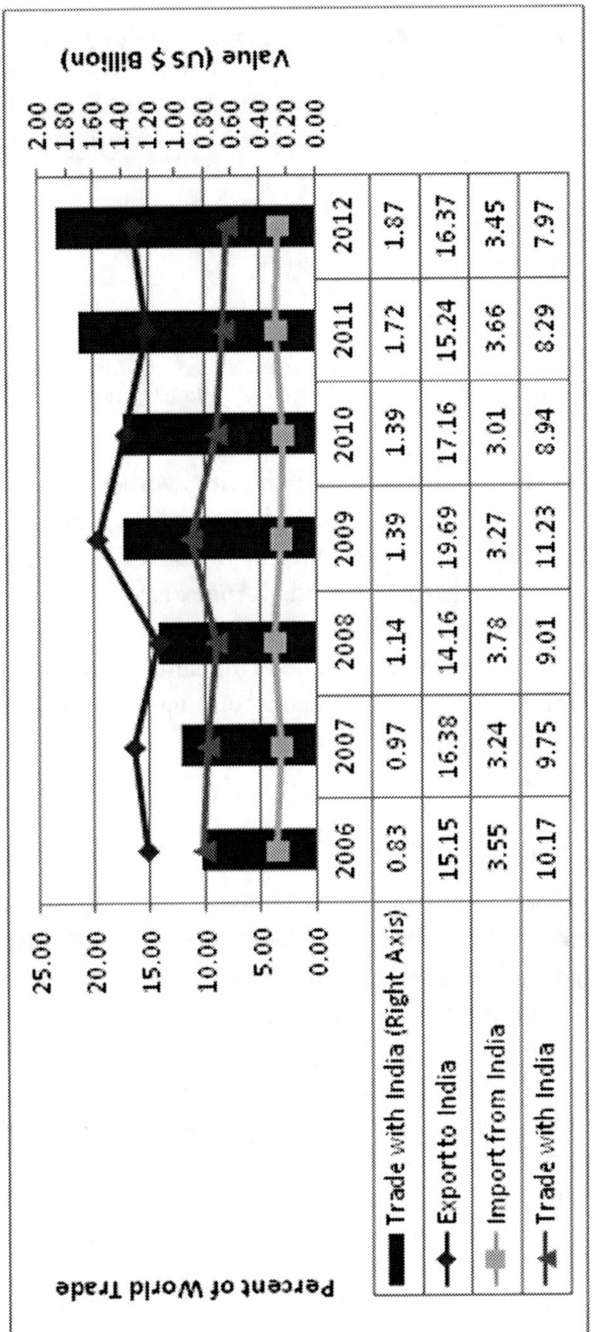

	2006	2007	2008	2009	2010	2011	2012
Trade with India (Right Axis)	0.83	0.97	1.14	1.39	1.39	1.72	1.87
Export to India	15.15	16.38	14.16	19.69	17.16	15.24	16.37
Import from India	3.55	3.24	3.78	3.27	3.01	3.66	3.45
Trade with India	10.17	9.75	9.01	11.23	8.94	8.29	7.97

Source: Authors' estimate based on World Bank data, World Integrated Trade Solution (WITS) database.

Table Seven: Additional Market Access Frontier among India's Trading Partners for products with export potential of India's North East (Value in US$ Billions)

Trading Partners	*Top Five products*	*All products*
India Supplier: Bangladesh Market	3.43	7.76
Bangladesh Supplier: India Market	0.29	1.23
China Supplier: India Market	18.91	115.89
India Supplier: China Market	47.56	128.89
India Supplier: Myanmar Market	2.32	10.63
Myanmar Supplier: India Market	0.72	1.84

Source: Authors' estimate based on World Bank data, World Integrated Trade Solution (WITS) database.

India's AMAF on all products is highest with China, followed by Myanmar and Bangladesh. Amongst India's suppliers, China has by far the highest AMAF with India. Myanmar and Bangladesh, by contrast, have relatively much lower AMAF with India. Annex tables A.1-A.6 give details of products in which India and India's partners have highest AMAF with each other, and for the summed value of remaining products that match each other in terms of exports and corresponding imports. The tables also show the corresponding customs tariffs on these products where such data could be obtained.

Products of Export Potential to India's North East

A Report by Government of India, Ministry of Development of North Eastern Region, (2008) *North Eastern Region: Vision 2020*[4], identified eight horticultural and mineral products of export potential to the NER. These are pineapples, oranges, bamboos, limestone, cement, citronella oil, cinnamon and natural rubber. The study makes an appraisal of AMAF of these products for India, presuming that India's North East could take advantage of this, being in the vicinity of these countries. India's export markets in this context include Bangladesh, Myanmar and Thailand. There are no exports to China. Thailand as a market has been considered, being a neighboring country and with a common membership under BIMSTEC. In addition to value of exports, the quantities to be exported are also indicated so as to consider this in context of available/enabling infrastructure to move the products. A summary of India's AMAF in these products is presented in Table 8.

Table Eight: India's Existing and Additional Market Access Frontier for Horticultural/Mineral Products: 2010 (Value in US$ '000, Qty in tones)

Products/Commodities	*Existing Exports*	*Additional Market Access Frontier*
Pineapples	25 (123)	68
Oranges	4954 (24076)	3479
Bamboos	13 (102)	60
Limestone	19496 (1907636)	3161
Cement	94 (1297)	40933
Citronella Oil	84 (3)	420
Cinnamon	349 (8)	
Natural Rubber	127 (51)	679

Note: Figures in brackets are quantities (unit: tonnes).
Source: Authors' estimate based on World Bank data, World Integrated Trade Solution (WITS) database.

The table above summarises the Additional Market Access Frontier (AMAF) of horticultural and mineral product exports by India to the BCIM region and Thailand. It will be seen that India's AMCF was in cement, Myanmar being the chief market (Table A.11) (Table A.8). Next in importance are oranges, the chief market being Thailand. In limestone, India can get additional market access in Bangladesh. In citronella oil, additional market access for India's North East is possible in Thailand and Myanmar (Table A.10). Annex tables A.7-A.12 give details.

Trade Restrictions in BCIM Countries

In this section, we examine trade restrictions in BCIM member countries in terms of Most-Favoured Nation (MFN) applied rates and also in terms of final bound[5] rates. In table Eight, it can be seen that while the average applied rates for all goods are highest in Bangladesh and India, those in

Myanmar and China are the lowest. The average applied rates for agricultural goods are generally higher than those on non-agricultural goods. The highest applied rates for agricultural goods are highest for India and lowest in Myanmar. For non-agricultural goods, the highest is in Bangladesh, followed by India, China and Myanmar.

The bound rates are highest in Bangladesh, followed by Myanmar, India and China. For agricultural goods, the highest bound rates are that of Bangladesh, followed by India, Myanmar and China. For non-agricultural goods, the highest rates are again in Bangladesh, followed by India, Myanmar and China. In general, it may be noted that both China and Myanmar have lower applied and bound tariff rates as compared to Bangladesh and India.

Annex Tables A.1 to A.14, while analysing the potential exportable products have, wherever available, also indicated customs tariffs applicable on them. Preferential tariff rates have also been indicated, wherever applicable or available. Where customs duties are high, member states may consider reducing the same either within a trade liberalisation framework to be adopted, or elsewhere in other regional preferential trading organisations of which they are members[6].

Intra-industry Trade in BCIM Region

Intra-industry trade (IIT) shows to what extent countries trade (export and import) with each other in similar products. When this happens, and industry moves to the country with the greatest opportunity to manufacture a product, horizontal integration takes place, taking advantage of economies of scale. To take note of possibilities of investment flows that take advantage of this integration, this paper examines the Grubel Llyod Index of intra-industry trade of India with other BCIM countries(see technical Appendix Two for definition).

Table A.15 shows India's IIT with Bangladesh. It can be seen that India imports and exports a number of textile products to Bangladesh falling under Standard Industrial Trade Classification[7] (6523, 6552, 6522). This points to the possibility of India setting up integrated textile mills in Bangladesh, both for export to India as well as to third countries.

India's IIT with China is shown in Annex Table (A.15).The industries in which China can invest in India and those in which India can invest in China are shown in the table. To illustrate, while China can set up industries in portable data processing machines (SITC 7522), telephone sets (SITC

Table Eight: Applied MFN Tariff of BCIM Countries Chart Title

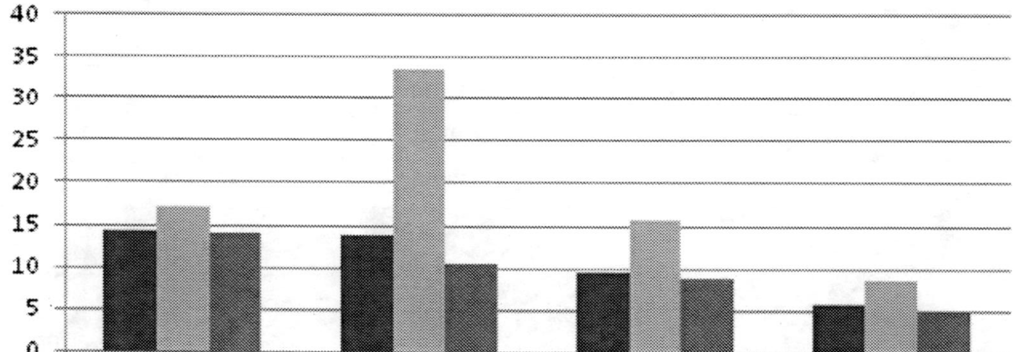

	Bangladesh (2011)	India (2012)	China (2011)	Myanmar (2012)
All goods	14.4	13.7	9.6	5.6
Agricultural goods (AOA)	17.2	33.5	15.6	8.6
Non-agricultural goods	14	10.4	8.7	5.1

Source: Authors' estimate based on World Bank data, World Integrated Trade Solution (WITS) database.

Table Nine: Final Bound Tariff Rates of BCIM Countries

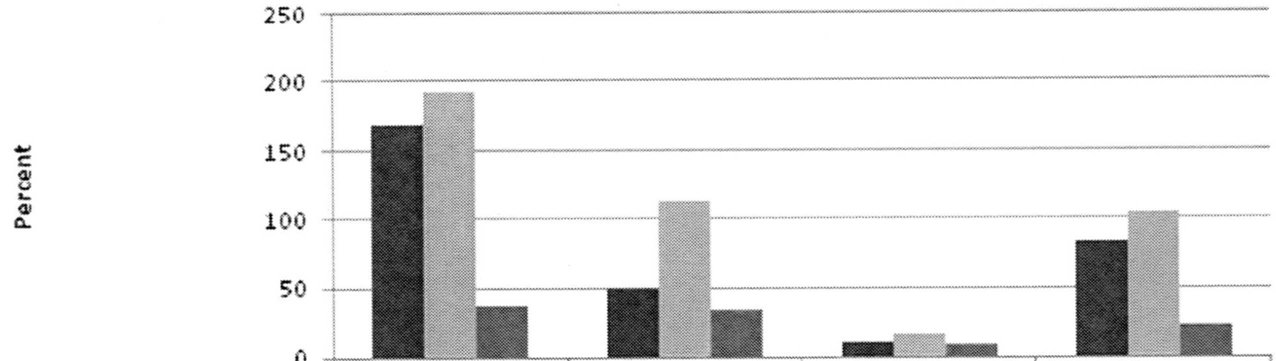

	Bangladesh	India	China	Myanmar
All goods	169.2	48.6	10	83.4
Agricultural goods (AOA)	192	113.1	15.8	103.7
Non-agricultural goods	37.3	34.5	9.1	21.8

Source: Authors' estimate based on World Bank data, World Integrated Trade Solution (WITS) database.

7641), etc., India can invest in cyclic hydrocarbons (SITC 5112), polymers of propylene (SITC 5751), petroleum refinery (SITC 3346), castor oils and its fractions (SITC 4225) etc. Table A.16 shows India's IIT with Myanmar. There appears to be absence of bulk trading in similar products. However, there seems to be some scope for Indian investment in motor vehicle parts (SITC 7843), machine tools (SITC 7331) and medicaments (SITC 5411).

Concluding Observations

There has been phenomenal growth in trade amongst BCIM member states, particularly amongst least developed countries like Bangladesh and Myanmar. Both India and China provide vast markets for these countries. Similarly, both India and China are vast markets for each other's products as well. This paper has identified in which India can have the highest additional market in partner countries and vice versa. A similar exercise has been done for estimating additional market access frontier for horticultural and mineral products in India's North East. Wherever available, tariff levels in destination countries have been provided to address such barriers when found to be high.

NOTES

1. Earlier study on trade flows was from 2000 to 2005 by CPD (1997). As of now, the last year of data availability is 2012.
2. www.wits.worldbank.org
3. To illustrate, Bangladesh's exports to China/India is China/India's imports from Bangladesh. Similarly, Bangladesh's imports from China/India are the latter countries' exports to Bangladesh. Bangladesh's world exports is all countries' imports from Bangladesh and Bangladesh's world imports is all countries' exports to Bangladesh.
4. Government of India, Ministry of Development of North Eastern Region, *North Eastern Region: Vision 2020,* http://mdoner.gov.in/sites/default/files/silo2_content/ner_vision/Vision_2020.pdf.
5. These rates are those communicated to WTO that member countries have pledged not to increase beyond.
6. For instance, Bangladesh, China, India are members of Asia Pacific Trade Agreement (APTA) while Bangladesh, Myanmar, India are members of BIMSTEC.
7. Standard Industrial Trade Classification is more appropriate for analysis of intra-industry trade.

Annex Tables

Table A.1: India Supplier: Bangladesh Market (2012, '000 US$)

Product Code	*Product Description*	*India's World Exports (Supply)*	*World Exports to Bangladesh (Demand)*	*India's Exports to Bangladesh*	*Additional Market Access Frontier*	*MFN Rate*	*Preferential Rate*
1	*2*	*3*	*4*	*5*	*6 = (min 3,4)-5*	*7*	*8*
271000	Petroleum oils and oils obtained from bituminous minerals, other than crude; preparations not elsewhere specified or included, containing by weight 70% or more of petroleum oils or of oils obtained from bituminous minerals	52,763,870	1,912,234	35,627	1,876,607	5%	NA
170111	Raw sugar not containing added flavouring or colouring matter: Cane sugar	1,008,701	776,229	219,448	556,781	2000/t	NA
520100	Cotton, not carded or combed.	3,647,065	962,197	542,878	419,319	5%	NA
852520	Transmission apparatus incorporating reception apparatus	2,860,506	258,097	0	258,097	5%	NA
100190	Seed, White, Other	739,215	350,830	119,493	231,337	5%	
Top 5 Products					3,342,141		
All 4,151 Products					7,763,093		

Source: Authors' estimate based on World Bank data, World Integrated Trade Solution (WITS) database.

Table A.2: Bangladesh Supplier: India Market (2012, '000 US$)

Product Code	*Product Description*	*World Imports from Bangladesh (Supply)*	*India's Imports from World (Demand)*	*India's Existing Imports from Bangladesh*	*Additional Market Access Frontier*	*MFN Rate**	*Preferential Rate**
1	*2*	*3*	*4*	*5*	*6 = (min 3,4)-5*	*7*	*8*
271000	Petroleum oils and oils obtained from bituminous minerals, other than crude; preparations not elsewhere specified or included, containing by weight 70% or more of petroleum oils or of oils obtained from bituminous minerals	139,374	5,172,377	20,396	118,977	10%	0%
410439	Other bovine leather and equine leather, parchment-dressed or prepared after tanning: Other	49,592	162,954	2,705	46,887	10%	0%
871200	Bicycles and other cycles (including delivery tricycles), not motorised	65,488	41,685	84	41,601	10%	0%
640399	Other Footwear With Uppers of Leather	149,830	41,541	256	41,284	10%	0%
391590	Waste, Parings, Scrap of Other Plastics	40,395	100,064	0	40,395	10%	0%
Top 5					**289,144**		
All 2,150 Products					**1,232,312**		

*Indian customs.

Source: Authors' estimate based on World Bank data, World Integrated Trade Solution (WITS) database.

Table A.3: China Supplier: India Market (2012, '000 US$)

Product Code	*Product Description*	*China World Export (Supply)*	*India World Import (Demand)*	*China Export to India (Existing Exports)*	*Additional Market Access Frontier*	*MFN Rate*	*Preferential Rate*
1	*2*	*3*	*4*	*5*	*6 = (min 3,4)-5*	*7*	*8*
271000	Petroleum oils and oils obtained from bituminous minerals, other than crude; preparations not elsewhere specified or included, containing by weight 70% or more of petroleum oils or of oils obtained from bituminous minerals	21,316,334	5,172,377	29,470	5,142,906	10%	0%
711319	Of precious metal whether or not plated or clad with precious metal: Of other precious metal, whether or not plated or clad with precious metal	22,209,234	5,088,330	369	5,087,961	10%	0%
852520	Transmission apparatus incorporating reception apparatus	81,472,029	4,631,606	1,040,429	3,591,177	8%	8%
710239	Other Nonindustrial Diamond	2,872,484	6,300,566	4,155	2,868,328	10%	8%
270900	Petroleum oils and oils obtained from bituminous minerals, crude	2,226,025	148,757,013	0	2,226,025	5%	5%
Top 5 Products					**18,916,397**		
All 3,636 Products					**115,896,124**		

* Indian customs.

Source: Authors' estimate based on World Bank data, World Integrated Trade Solution (WITS) database.

Table A.4: India Supplier: China Market (2012, '000 US$)

Product Code	*Product Description*	*India's World Exports (Supply)*	*China imports from World (Demand)*	*India's Exports to China*	*Additional Market Access Frontier*
1	*2*	*3*	*4*	*5*	*6 = (min 3,4)-5*
271000	Petroleum oils and oils obtained from bituminous minerals, other than crude; preparations not elsewhere specified or included, containing by weight 70% or more of petroleum oils or of oils obtained from bituminous minerals, these oils	52,763,870	33,033,167	307,427	32,725,741
300490	Other Medicaments (Put up in Packings for Retail Sale)	6,631,780	6,523,806	4,520	6,519,286
710239	Other Nonindustrial Diamond	20,819,464	4,226,239	74,072	4,152,167
870899	Other parts and accessories for motor vehicles	2,528,996	2,889,945	36,311	2,492,684
852520	Transmission apparatus incorporating reception apparatus	2,860,506	1,677,643	1,109	1,676,534
Top 5 Products					47,566,412
All 4,372 Products					128,891,095

Note: Customs tariff for China n/a.
Source: Authors' estimate based on World Bank data, World Integrated Trade Solution (WITS) database.

Table A.5: India Supplier: Myanmar Market (2012, US$ '000)

Product Code	*Product Description*	*India's Export to World (Supply)*	*World Export to Myanmar (Demand)*	*India's Existing Export to Myanmar*	*Additional Market Access Frontier*	*MFN Rate**	*Preferential Rate**
1	*2*	*3*	*4*	*5*	*6 = (min 3,4)-5*	*7*	*8*
271000	Petroleum oils and oils obtained from bituminous minerals, other than crude; preparations not elsewhere specified or included, containing by weight 70% or more of petroleum oils or of oils obtained from bituminous minerals	52,763,870	1,070,408	1,832	1,068,576	1.5%	1.5%
730890	Other Structures and Parts of Structures, of Iron or Steel	394,209	801,549	3,931	390,279	n/a	n/a
871120	With reciprocating internal combustion piston engine of a cylinder capacity exceeding 50cc but not exceeding 250cc	1,284,825	342,361	0	342,361	n/a	n/a
870323	Other vehicles, with spark-ignition internal combustion reciprocating piston engine: Of a cylinder capacity exceeding 1,500cc but not exceeding 3,000cc	363,143	259,297	37	259,260	n/a	n/a
730511	Line pipe of a kind used for oil or gas pipe-lines: Longitudinally submerged arc welded	1,291,417	339,782	82,595	257,187	n/a	n/a
Top 5					**2,317,663**		
All 3,763 Products					**10,631,253**		

*Myanmar customs.

Source: Authors' estimate based on World Bank data, World Integrated Trade Solution (WITS) database.

Table A.6: Myanmar Supplier: India Market (2012, '000 US$)

Product Code	*Product Description*	*World Imports from Myanmar (Supply)*	*India imports from World (Demand)*	*Myanmar's Exports to India*	*Additional Market Access Frontier*	*MFN Rate**	*Preferential Rate**
1	*2*	*3*	*4*	*5*	*6 = (min 3,4)-5*	*7*	*8*
440349	Other, of tropical wood specified in Subheading Note 1 to this Chapter: Other	510,555	740,815	334,441	176,114	5%	5%
710310	Precious stones - Unworked or simply sawn or roughly shaped	159,659	296,498	0	159,659	10%	10%
440399	Other - wood in the rough, stripped or not of sapwood etc	493,101	1,203,372	334,950	158,151	5%	5%
400121	Natural rubber in other forms: Smoked sheets	115,781	434,456	202	115,579	25%	25%
071331	Beans (Vigna spp., Phaseolus spp.): Beans of the species Vigna mungo (L.) Hepper or Vigna radiata (L.) Wilczek	384,743	390,700	272,180	112,564	30%	30%
Top 5 Products					**722,066**		
All 1,655 Products					**1,841,134**		

*Indian customs.

Source: Authors' estimate based on World Bank data, World Integrated Trade Solution (WITS) database.

Table A.7: India's Additional Market Access Frontier in Pineapples (2010)

			Partner		
			Bangladesh	*Myanmar*	*Thailand*
Value in Thousand US$	1	India's World Exports	855	855	855
	2	Partner's World Imports	28	1	64
	3	Existing Exports	25	0	0
	4	Additional Market Access Frontier = min (1,2)-3	3	1	64
Quantity in Tonnes	1	India's World Exports	3,858	3,858	3,858
	2	Partner's World Imports	128	1	61
	3	Existing Exports	123	0	0
Custom Duty		MFN Rate		15%	60%
		Preferential Rate		15%	12%
		Source		Myanmar Customs	Thailand Customs

Source: Authors' estimate based on World Bank data, World Integrated Trade Solution (WITS) database.

Table A.8: India's Additional Market Access Frontier in Oranges (2010)

			Partner		
			Bangladesh	*Myanmar*	*Thailand*
Value in Thousand US$	1	India's World Exports	5,527	5,527	5,527
	2	Partner's World Imports	16,778	614	2,292
	3	Existing Exports	4,954	0	0
	4	Additional Market Access Frontier = (min 1,2)-3	573	614	2,292
Quantity in Tonnes	1	India's World Exports	26,885	26,885	26,885
	2	Partner's World Imports	54,893	1,114	2,941
	3	Existing Exports	24,076	0	0
	4	Additional Market Access Frontier = min (1,2)-3	2809	1,114	9412,
Custom Duty		MFN Rate		15%	60%
		Preferential Rate		15%	0%
		Source		Myanmar Customs	Thailand Customs

Source: Authors' estimate based on World Bank data, World Integrated Trade Solution (WITS) database.

Table A.9: India's Additional Market Access Frontier in Bamboos (2010)

			Partner		
			Bangladesh	*Myanmar*	*Thailand*
Value in Thousand US$	1	India's World Exports	60	60	60
	2	Partner's World Imports	13	5	55
	3	Existing Trade	13	0	0
	4	Additional Market Access Frontier = (min 1,2)-3	0	5	55
Quantity in Tonnes		India's World Exports	268	268	268
		Partner's World Imports	102	5	101
		Existing Exports	102	0	0
Custom Duty		MFN Rate		5%	35%
		Preferential Rate		5%	0%
		Source		Myanmar Customs	Thailand Customs

Source: Authors' estimate based on World Bank data, World Integrated Trade Solution (WITS) database.

Table A.10: India's Additional Market Access Frontier in Limestone (2010)

			Partner		
			Bangladesh	*Myanmar*	*Thailand*
Value in Thousand US$	1	India's World Exports	24,203	24,203	24,203
	2	Partner's World Imports	22,110	13	184
	3	Existing Trade	19,049	0	87
	4	Additional Market Access Frontier = min (1,2)-3	3,061	13	97
Quantity in Tonnes		India's World Exports	1,980,676	1,980,676	1,980,676
		Partner's World Imports	1,978,939	105	2,409
		Existing Exports	1,906,576	0	1,060
Custom Duty		MFN Rate		1%	15%
		Preferential Rate		1%	0%
		Source		Myanmar Customs	Thailand Customs

Source: Authors' estimate based on World Bank data, World Integrated Trade Solution (WITS) database.

Table A.11: India's Additional Market Access Frontier in Cement (2010)

			Partner		
			Bangladesh	*Myanmar*	*Thailand*
Value in Thousand US$	1	India's World Exports	131,153	131,153	131,153
	2	Partner's World Imports	105	39,074	1,848
	4	Existing Exports	94	0	0
	4	Additional Market Access Frontier = min (1,2)-3	11	39,074	1,848
Quantity in Tonnes		India's World Exports	2,100,910	2,100,910	2,100,910
		Partner's World Imports	1,342	701,484	42,861
		Existing Exports	1,297	0	0
Custom Duty		MFN Rate		1%	30%
		Preferential Rate		1%	6%
		Source		Myanmar Customs	Thailand Customs

Source: Authors' estimate based on World Bank data, World Integrated Trade Solution (WITS) database.

Table A.12: India's Additional Market Access Frontier in Citronella Oil (2010)

			Partner		
			Bangladesh	*Myanmar*	*Thailand*
Value in Thousand US$	1	India's World Exports	6,063	6,063	6,063
	2	Partner's World Imports	29	208	266
	3	Existing exports	27	53	4
	4	Additional Market Access Frontier= MIN (1,2)-3	2	155	263
Quantity in Tonnes		India's World Exports	229	229	229
		Partner's World Imports	1	16	10
		Existing Exports	1	2	0
Custom Duty		MFN Rate		n/a	35%
		Preferential Rate		n/a	0%
		Source			Thailand Customs

Source: Authors' estimate based on World Bank data, World Integrated Trade Solution (WITS) database.

Table A.13: India's Additional Market Access Frontier in Cinnamon (2010)

			Partner		
			Bangladesh	*Myanmar*	*Thailand*
Value in Thousand US$	1	India's World Exports	34,687	34,687	34,687
	2	Partner's World Imports	203	412	3,616
	3	Existing Exports	157	12	180
	4	Additional Market Access Frontier = min (1,2)-3	46	400	3,436
Quantity in Tonnes		India's World Exports	971	971	971
		Partner's World Imports	5	90	197
		Existing Exports	3	0	5
Custom Duty		MFN Rate		3%	30%
		Preferential Rate		3%	0%
		Source		Myanmar Customs	Thailand Customs

Source: Authors' estimate based on World Bank data, World Integrated Trade Solution (WITS) database.

Table A.14: India's Additional Market Access Frontier in Natural Rubber (2010)

			Partner		
			Bangladesh	*Myanmar*	*Thailand*
Value in Thousand US$	1	India's World Exports	26,498	26,498	26,498
	2	Partner's World Imports	650	8	148
	3	Existing Exports	114	8	5
	4	Additional Market Access Frontier = min (1,2)-3	537	0	142
Quantity in Tonnes		India's World Exports	10,523	10,523	10,523
		Partner's World Imports	213	4	93
		Existing Exports	51	4	2
Custom Duty		MFN Rate		1%	0%
		Preferential Rate		1%	0%
		Source		Myanmar Customs	Thailand Customs

Source: Authors' estimate based on World Bank data, World Integrated Trade Solution (WITS) database.

Table A.15: India's Intra-Industry Trade with Bangladesh (2012, US$ '000)

Product Code	*Product Description*	*India's imports from Bangladesh*	*India's export to Bangladesh*	*Intra-Industry Trade*
6523	Other woven fabrics, containing 85% or more by weight of cotton, bleached, dyed, printed or otherwise finished, weighing not more than 200 g/m^2	10,413	94,275	19.9
6552	Other knitted or crocheted fabrics, not impregnated, coated, covered or laminated	2,059	37,152	10.5
3346	Petroleum oils & oils obtained from bituminous minerals (other than crude) & preparations n.e.s., containing by weight 70 %/more of petroleum oils/of oils obtained from bituminous minerals, these oils being the basic constituents of the preparations	20,395	35,561	72.9
6522	Cotton fabrics, woven, unbleached (other than gauze and pile and chenille fabrics)	1,052	8,358	22.4
7781	Batteries and electric accumulators and parts thereof	1,627	6,093	42.2
6114	Tanned or crust hides and skins of bovine (including buffalo) or equine animals whether or not further prepared after tanning or crusting, without hair on, whether or not split	3,292	5,718	73.1
5226	Other inorganic bases and metal oxides, hydroxides and peroxides	16,794	5,478	49.2
8931	Articles for the conveyance or packing of goods, of plastics; stoppers, lids, caps and other closures, of plastics	3,212	5,030	77.9
8412	Suits and ensembles	2,275	4,321	69.0
5711	Polyethylene	1,402	4,267	49.5

(*Contd.*)

Table A.15: (*Contd.*)

Product Code	*Product Description*	*India's imports from Bangladesh*	*India's export to Bangladesh*	*Intra-Industry Trade*
8933	Floor coverings, wall or ceiling coverings and household and toilet articles of plastics	1,056	3,335	48.1
6589	Made-up articles of textile materials, n.e.s.	2,779	2,803	99.6
2734	Pebbles, gravel, broken/crushed stone, of a kind commonly used for concrete aggregates, for road metalling/for railway/other ballast, shingle & flint, whether/not heat-treated; macadam of slag, dross/similar industrial waste, whether or not incorporating	9,916	2,703	42.8
8451	Babies' garments and clothing accessories	1,072	2,520	59.7
8415	Shirts	19,964	2,087	18.9
6851	Lead and lead alloys, unwrought	3,502	1,702	65.4
6861	Zinc and zinc alloys, unwrought	4,832	1,516	47.8
7614	Other monitors	2,669	1,454	70.5
8453	Jerseys, pullovers, cardigans, waistcoats & similar articles, knitted/crocheted	1,905	975	67.7
6585	Curtains and other furnishing articles, n.e.s., of textile materials	1,019	835	90.1
6612	Portland cement, aluminous cement, slag cement, supersulphate cement and similar hydraulic cements, whether or not coloured or in the form of clinkers.	15,743	625	7.6

Source: Authors' estimate based on World Bank data, World Integrated Trade Solution (WITS) database.

Table A.16: India's Intra-Industry Trade with China (2012, US$ '000)

Product Code	*Product Description*	*India's imports from China*	*India's export to China*	*Total Trade*	*Intra-Industry Trade*	*Investment by China*	*Investment by India*
1	*2*	*3*	*4*	*5*	*6*	*7*	*8*
7522	Portable automatic data processing machines, weighing not > 10 kg, consisting of a least a central processing unit, a keyboard & a display	1,678,503	755	1,679,258	0.1	/	
7641	Telephone sets, including telephones for cellular networks or for other wireless networks; other apparatus for the transmission or reception of voice, images or other data, including apparatus for communication in a wired or wireless network (such as a 1)	5,843,159	86,600	5,929,759	2.9	/	
5629	Fertilizers, n.e.s.	1,559,414	4	1,559,418	0.0	/	
7599	Parts and accessories (other than covers, carrying cases and the like) suitable for use solely or principally with the machines of subgroups 751.1, 751.2, 751.9 and group 752	789,732	48,887	838,619	11.7	/	
5169	Organic chemicals, n.e.s.	692,604	42,883	735,487	11.7	/	
5413	Antibiotics, not put up as medicaments of group 542	664,190	42,457	706,647	12.0	/	
6791	Tubes, pipes and hollow profiles, seamless, of iron or steel	620,614	16,455	637,069	5.2	/	
5157	Other heterocyclic compounds; nucleic acids	569,759	44,462	614,221	14.5	/	

(*Contd.*)

1	2	3	4	5	6	7	8
7843	Other parts and accessories of the motor vehicles of groups 722, 781, 782 and 783	543,546	63,385	606,931	20.9	/	
7649	Parts and accessories suitable for use solely or principally with the apparatus of division 76	541,303	11,981	553,284	4.3	/	
7763	Diodes, transistors and similar semiconductor devices; photosensitive semiconductor devices (including photovoltaic cells, whether or not assembled in modules or made up into panels); light-emitting diodes	505,710	3,731	509,441	1.5	/	
2731	Building or monumental (dimension) stone, not further worked than roughly trimmed or merely cut, by sawing or otherwise, into blocks or slabs of a rectangular (including square) shape	4,308	490,421	494,728	1.74		/
7519	Other office machines (e.g., hectograph or stencil-duplicating machines, addressing machines, automatic banknote dispensers, coin-sorting machines, coin-counting or wrapping machines, pencil-sharpening machines, perforating or stapling machines); other p	463,289	381	463,670	0.16	/	
7781	Batteries and electric accumulators and parts thereof	460,439	1,653	462,092	0.72	/	
7712	Other electric power machinery; parts of the electric power machinery of group 771	439,817	21,938	461,754	9.5	/	

(*Contd.*)

1	2	3	4	5	6	7	8
8984	Discs, tapes, solid-state non-volatile storage devices, smart cards and other media for the recording of sound or of other phenomena, whether or not recorded, including matrices and masters for the production of discs, but excluding products of group	451,662	6,569	458,231	2.87	/	
5112	Cyclic hydrocarbons	56,454	360,592	417,046	27.07		/
7616	Reception apparatus for television, whether/not incorporating radio-broadcast receivers/sound/ video recording/reproducing apparatus	425,971	24	425,996	0.0	/	
5751	Polymers of propylene or of other olefins	25,550	393,054	418,604	12.2		/
5112	Cyclic hydrocarbons	56,454	360,592	417,046	27.1		/
6715	Other ferro-alloys (excluding radioactive ferro-alloys)	57,513	312,020	369,533	31.1		/
3346	Petroleum oils & oils obtained from bituminous minerals (other than crude) & preparations n.e.s., containing by weight 70%/more of petroleum oils/ of oils obtained from bituminous minerals, these oils being the basic constituents of the preparations, oth	44,825	307,427	352,252	25.5		/
4225	Castor oil & its fractions	66	316,070	316,136	0.0		/
2929	Materials of vegetable origin, n.e.s.	14,667	296,826	311,493	9.4		/
5123	Cyclic alcohols and their halogenated, sulphonated, nitrated or nitrosated derivatives	25,314	235,938	261,252	19.4		/

(*Contd.*)

1	*2*	*3*	*4*	*5*	*6*	*7*	*8*
5513	Essential oils (terpeneless or not), including concretes and absolutes; resinoids; concentrates of essential oils in fats, in fixed oils, in waxes or the like, obtained by enfleurage of maceration; terpenic by-products of the deterpenation of essential	36,409	135,959	172,369	42.3		/
2852	Alumina (aluminium oxide), other than artificial corundum	40,899	42,270	83,169	98.4		/

Source: Authors' estimate based on World Bank data, World Integrated Trade Solution (WITS) database.

Table A.16: India's Intra-Industry Trade with Myanmar

Product Code	*Product Description*	*India's imports from Myanmar*	*India's export to Myanmar*	*Intra-Industry Trade*
7843	Other parts and accessories of the motor vehicles of groups 722, 781, 782 and 783	1,341	1,336	99.8
2919	Materials of animal origin, n.e.s.	1,376	1,363	99.5
752	Spices (except pepper and pimento)	2,088	2,715	87.0
5741	Polyacetals and other polyethers	106	100	97.0
5411	Provitamins and vitamins, natural or reproduced by synthesis (including natural concentrates), derivatives thereof used primarily as vitamins, and intermixtures of the foregoing, whether or not in any solvent, not put up as medicaments of group 542	165	175	96.9
6942	Screws, bolts, nuts, coach screws, screw hooks, rivets, cotters, cotter pins, washers (including spring washers) and similar articles, of iron or steel	149	173	92.6
752	Spices (except pepper and pimento)	2,088	2,715	87.0
7331	Machine tools (including presses) for working metal by forging, hammering or die-stamping; machine tools (including presses) for working metal by bending, folding, straightening, flattening, shearing, punching or notching; presses for working metal or me	1,298	733	72.2
5137	Monocarboxylic acids and their anhydrides, halides, peroxides and peroxyacids; their halogenated, sulphonated, nitrated or nitrosated derivatives	848	215	40.4
3346	Petroleum oils & oils obtained from bituminous minerals (other than crude) & preparations n.e.s., containing by weight 70 %/more of petroleum oils/of oils obtained from bituminous minerals, these oils being the basic constituents of the preparations	10,493	1,832	29.7

Source: Authors' estimate based on World Bank data, World Integrated Trade Solution (WITS) database.

Technical Appendix 1

Definition: Market Access Frontier (trade potential):

Market Access Frontier for product i is given as:

$$\sum_{i=1}^{n} (\min SEi, MIi) - ETi$$

Where:

SEi = Supplier's Global Exports of product i;

MIi = Market's Global Imports of product i;

ETi = Supplier's Existing Exports of product i to Partner's Market.

Technical Appendix 2

The **Grubel-Lloyd index** measures intra-industry trade of a particular product. It was introduced by Herb Grubel and Peter Lloyd in 1971.

$$GL_i = \frac{(M_i + M_i) - |X_i - M_i|}{X_i + M_i} = 1 - \frac{|X_i - M_i|}{X_i + M_i}\ ; 0 < GL_i < 1$$

where X_i denotes the export, M_i the import of good i.

If $GL_i = 1$, there is only intra-industry trade, no inter-industry trade. This means, for example, the country in consideration exports same quantity of goods i as it imports. Conversely, if $GL_i = 0$, there is no intra-industry trade, only inter-industry trade. This would mean that the country in consideration only either exports or only imports good i.

4

Sub-Regional Cooperation for the Development of Landlocked Peripheral Areas: The Case of BCIM

Gurudas Das, Ujjwal K Paul and Tanuj Mathur

Development of peripheries has always been a major challenge to large States. Peripheries are border areas which are far away from the mainland and national market hubs. One of the reasons for the underdevelopment of peripheral border areas is the traditional state-centric security perception. For example, the traditional "Scorched Earth" Policy, a policy of keeping the borders deliberately underdeveloped so that enemy forces cannot make any sweeping progress adopted by most states during the pre-missile era, has been one of the reasons for the underdevelopment of bordering regions.

Moreover, as peripheries are often inhabited by minority groups, skewed minority representation in decision-making weakens their bargaining power over allocation of federal resources in a democratic federal structure. Thus, state-led development suffers from a built-in bias against peripheral areas. Besides the weak bargaining power of minority groups, peripheral development is also shaped by the external security threat perception of states, which discourages large public sector investment in these areas. In addition, the logic of limited spread also impacts negatively on policy decisions on public sector investments in peripheral areas.

Infrastructure deficit also discourages private investment in these areas. Lack of physical and institutional infrastructure, in turn, stands in the way of regionalisation of production, consumption and market formation. Whatever limited public investment is made through statutory channels, the income generated in the process is nevertheless spent on the procurement of necessities from the mainland, forcing peripheral economies to operate at sub-optimal levels. High cost of production, higher transportation costs and skill deficit do not allow peripheral economies to grow in line with their respective perceived comparative advantage. Thus, market-led growth bypasses these areas.

Peripheral growth is driven by the need for national development. Resource exploitation in peripheral areas warrants first, the scarcity of a particular natural resource product to go up to such a level that it can justify higher prices at which it can be supplied in the national market. Market signals from the national economy are not strong enough to bring resources available in peripheral areas—except the critical ones—into immediate use. Here lies the theoretical rationale to look beyond the framework of the national economy and the state-centric mindset while formulating the development strategy for border areas like the NER and China's South West.

Sub-regional cooperation across international borders has been used as a strategy to promote growth and development of peripheral areas in different parts of the globe. The success of sub-regional groupings like (i) "Southern China Growth Triangle" involving Guangdong and Fujian provinces of China, Taiwan and Hong Kong, (ii) "Southern Growth Triangle" (SIJORI) involving Singapore, Johor state of Malaysia, and Indonesian island of Batam in the province of Riau, (iii) "Greater Mekong Sub-Region" (GMS) involving Yunnan province of China, Vietnam, Laos, Cambodia, Thailand and Myanmar; (iv) Indonesia, Malaysia and Thailand Growth Triangle (IMT-GT) involving Sumatra in Indonesia, peninsular Malaysia and Southern Thailand, and (v) Greater Tumen Initiative (GTI) involving four provinces of China, four Eastern port cities of Republic of Korea (ROK), three provinces of Mongolia and Russia's Far East, to name a few, have proved the efficacy of this strategy as a means of promoting peripheral areas beyond doubt.

2. Sub-Regional Cooperation for Development: Case Studies

Before we deal with the BCIM as a tool for development of underdeveloped areas in constituent countries, a brief account of five such sub-regional groupings and their contribution to development of the concerned sub-regions are in order.

2.1 Greater Mekong Sub-Region

Started as an ambitious initiative of the Asian Development Bank (ADB) in 1992, GMS has seen an investment of nearly US$ 15 billion by June 2012.[1] The GMS consists of five triangle areas, of which two are located on river Mekong and three on land. The six member countries of GMS are Cambodia, the Lao People's Democratic Republic (Lao PDR), Myanmar, Thailand, Vietnam, Yunnan Province and Guangxi Zhuang Autonomous region in the People's Republic of China (PRC). Of these countries, PRC has grown by 10.3 per cent, while the remaining countries have grown by 5.3 per cent over 1992-2010.[2] During the initial years, GMS countries emphasised more on intra-regional "connectivity" than on "competitiveness" and "community"—the other two pillars of its vision.[3] With reasonable progress made on the 'hardware' aspect of integration by way of building three flagship GMS economic corridors—East-West, North-South and the Southern — the GMS power integration project, telecom connections using optical fiber interconnections and with work progressing towards incorporating broadband internet connectivity across the GMS sub-region, the members of the sub-region have now started to steer the 'software' aspects of integration, i.e., competitiveness and community to complement advancements made in the hardware component.[4] Through the past two decades, sub-regional GDP has grown over eight per cent while the per capita income has tripled.[5]

China emerges as the biggest beneficiary of the GMS sub-regional grouping. The trade between GMS and China has grown faster than the overall GMS-5 trade (except China). Manufacturing products share in this trade, is more than 2/3rd, both in exports and imports. The annual average exports of GMS countries have grown by 17.4 per cent during 2000-09. The annual average imports (including intra-GMS imports) for the same period has grown by 16.6 per cent. China, with a contribution of almost 85 per cent, has played a pivotal role in determining the growth of exports and imports in the region.[6]

Map One: Map of Greater Mekong Region

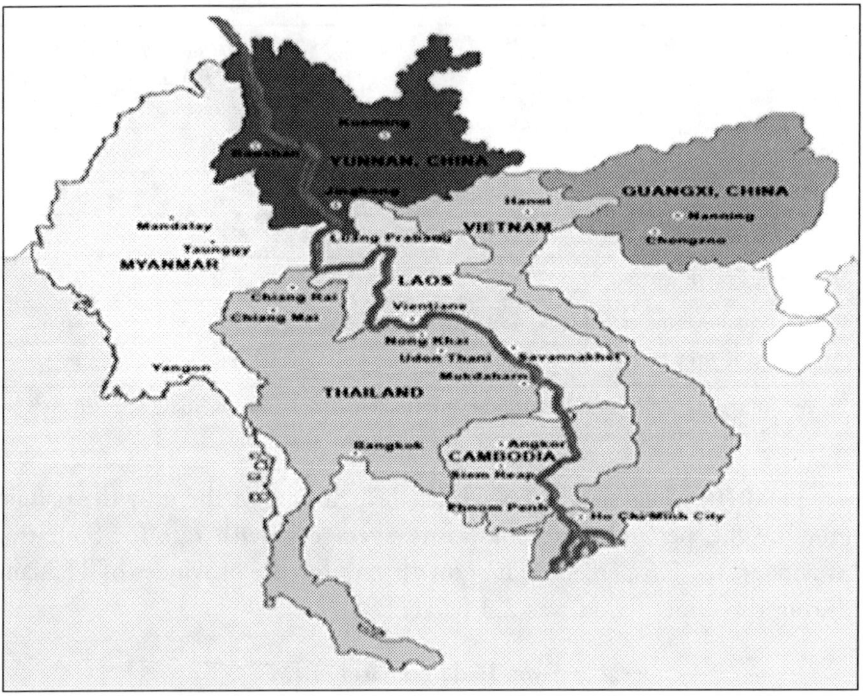

Source: www.mekongtourism.org

2.2 Indonesia-Malaysia-Thailand Growth Triangle

Launched in 1993 with the objective of transforming the economies of the peripheral region, the governments of Indonesia, Malaysia and Thailand have joined hands to set up the IMT-Growth Triangle (IMT-GT). Characterised by substantial socio-economic complementarity across borders, IMT-GT is considered to be a classic example of sub-regional integration for economic prosperity, attempting to serve the needs of nearly 75 million people living in a geographical area of 6.15 lakh sq km. Right from inception, this integration has expanded substantially in terms of size and scope. It includes 10 provinces of Sumatra region (Indonesia), eight states of Peninsular Malaysia and 14 provinces of Southern Thailand.[7]

Table One: Important Economic Indicators of IMT-GT

Parameters	*IMT-GT*	*As a percentage of overall IMT Nations Taken Together*	*Percent of ASEAN*
Population, 2011	75 million	22.4	12.5
Land area, 2011	6.15,lakhs sq. km	22.3	13.9
GDP at current prices, 2010	273,539US$ million	21.2	14.5
AGR of real GDP, 2010	6.4	6.9	7.8
Total international trade, 2011	489,375US$ million	39.1	20.5
Labour force, 2011	36,436'000	21.6	12.1

Source: imtgt.org/.../IMT-GT_Statistical_Information_Brief_Brochure.pdfý accessed on 22/1/2014

In 2010, Malaysian states which formed part of the growth triangle, grew by 8.6 percent. The composite average growth rate for Sumatran provinces was 5.6 percent. The growth rate for the provinces of Thailand during the same period was 2.3 percent.

Table Two: Trade Scenario of IMT-GT

IMT-GT Trade, 2011 (US$ billions)	*Intra-IMT-GT*	*Rest of the World*	*Total IMT-GT*
Exports	27,845	247,402	275,246
Imports	30,815	183,313	214,129

Source: imtgt.org/.../IMT-GT_Statistical_Information_Brief_Brochure.pdfý accessed on 22/1/2014

The principal traded commodities of IMT-GT include vegetables, rubber, petroleum oil, etc. for Indonesia, Thermionic valves and tubes, automatic data processing machines, telecommunication equipments, etc. for Malaysia and fish and fillets, rubber latex, albacore, etc. for Thailand.

Significant advances have been achieved on the infrastructure front as well with the extension and overhauling of rail, road, maritime and air connectivity in the growth triangle. In case of human resource development, IMT-GT has established UNINET-a cooperative form of education, research and exchange. The major chunk of investment comes from Malaysia, while Indonesia and Thailand provide access to other factors of production including labour, land and natural resources.[8]

Map Two: Map of IMT-GT

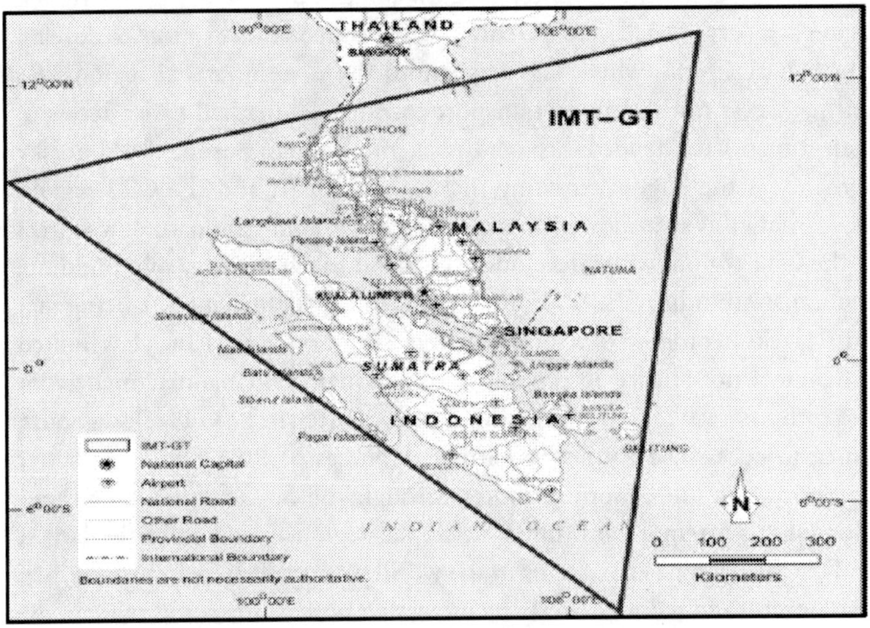

Source: www.imtgt.org/Documents/Books/roadmap-development.pdf

2.3 The Greater Tumen Initiative

The Greater Tumen Initiative—originally known as Tumen River Area Development Programme (TRADP)—is an inter-governmental regional cooperation mechanism in Northeast Asia, supported by the United Nations Development Programme (UNDP) and has a membership of four countries: China, Mongolia, ROK and Russian Federation.[9] It was initiated by UNDP in 1991. The objective of the initiative was to strengthen regional economic cooperation amongst member countries and develop the Northeast Asia (NEA) regional belt. The initiative was named after River 'Tumen', which flows along the border between North Korea and North East China and Far East Russia. The Greater Tumen Region (GTI) comprises four provinces of China viz. Heilongjiang, Inner Mongolia, Jilin and Liaoning; Eastern port cities of Republic of Korea like Busan, Ulsan, Gangwon-do and Gyeongsangbuk-do; three provinces of Mongolia viz. Hentii, Dornod and Sukhbaatar and Russia's Far East, i.e., Primorsky Territory.

China was the first country to show interest in developing the Tumen region as a part of its plan to use sub-regional cooperation as a tool to develop North East China, which lags far behind the eastern coastal regions. By getting access to the Tumen transport corridor, China had easier access to trade routes that extended through Russia into Western Europe.[10] Primorsky Territory is the largest economy in Far East Russia and the GTI region. Developing this area allowed Russia to access the abundant natural resources in the GTI region, while developing coal and metal mining, ship building, and transport industries. GTI provides the infrastructure and financing that Russia lacks in order to develop Primorsky Territory. South Korea has limited natural resources; hence, its economy depends mainly on manufactured goods and technology like semiconductors and computers. The GTI allows South Korea to access the abundant natural resources of Russia and the better transportation and shipping routes through the Sea of Japan.[11] Eastern Mongolia is a remote and underdeveloped region. It is one of the largest undisturbed Steppe ecosystems in the world. Mongolia hopes to strengthen its economy and reduce poverty by increasing both tourism and trade in the region through the Tumen transport corridor.

Map Three: Map of Greater Tumen Region

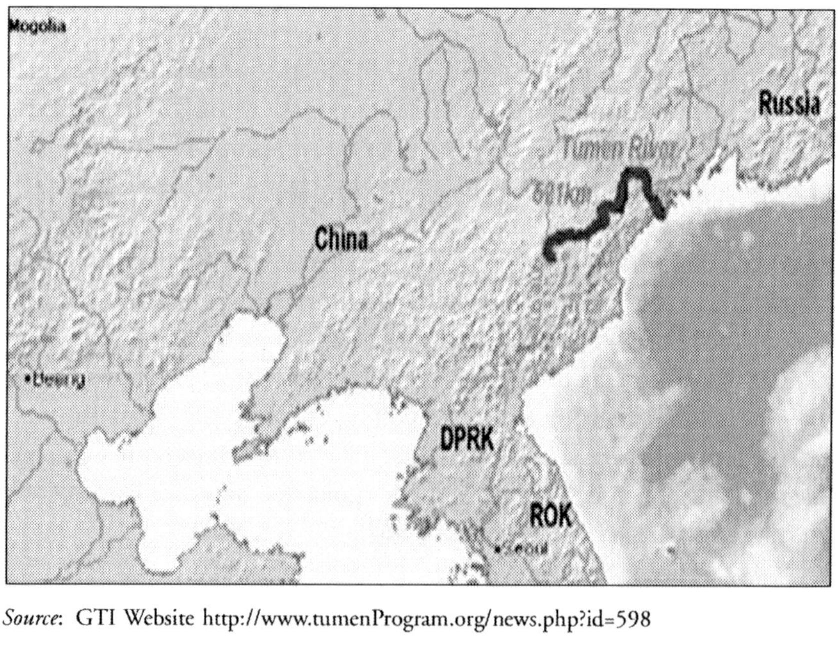

Source: GTI Website http://www.tumenProgram.org/news.php?id=598

Table Three: Greater Tumen Region at a Glance

Area	*Provinces*	*Population*	*GDP (Millions US$)*	*Main Industries*
North East China	Heilongjiang Province, Inner-Mongolia Region, Jilin Province, Liaoning Province	137,435,200	1,086,068 (2012)	Energy, Equipment, Petrochemicals, Pharmaceuticals, Automobiles, Iron & Steel, Textiles
Eastern Mongolia	Dornod Province, Khentii Province, Sukhbaatar Province	196,000	202 (2010)	Agriculture, Agri-processing, Mining, Tourism
Eastern ROK	Gangwon Province, Gyeongsangbuk Province, Busan City, Ulsan City	8,907,685	285,629 (2010)	Service Industry, Automobiles, Ship-building, Steel Production
Russian Far East	Primorsky Territory	1,948,873	18,559 (2011)	Energy, Light & Heavy Industry, Forestry & Timber, Tourism

Sources: http:// www.tumenprogramme.org/?list-1528.html

2.4 SIJORI – Singapore, Johor and Riau Growth Triangle (IMS-GT)

The SIJORI growth triangle is a partnership between Singapore, Johor (Malaysia) and Riau Islands (Indonesia). The agreement was reached to combine the competitive strengths of these areas as an attractive destination for regional and international investors. The SIJORI growth triangle was officially established in 1988, and was referred to as IMS-GT.[12] IMS-GT operates as a bilateral link to Singapore and Johor, Singapore and Riau Islands and Johor and Riau Islands. There is a high level of economic interaction between Singapore and Johor as they share geographical proximity. Johor is a significant source of water and power for Singapore. Singapore's labour intensive industries relocated to Johor to enhance their international competitiveness by leveraging lower production costs. Only minor commercial links exist between Johor and Riau. In 1993, Malaysia's Cabinet gave the state Government of Johor the prerogative to pursue direct bilateral links with Riau at a state/provincial level. Largely as a result of severe labour shortages, Johor is now looking at the possibility of encouraging companies in the plantation sector to invest in Indonesia.[13]

The SIJORI (IMS-GT) has led to accelerated investment in infrastructure and natural resource development, and also in export-oriented industrial and commercial development. This gives it the added benefits of income growth, structural change, employment creation, skills development and technology transfer in each of the areas involved. Riau has seen the greatest benefit since 1989; economic links with Singapore have helped transform Batam's economy, with rapid increases in population and strong positive trends in most indicators of economic development. Also, development is spreading to other islands in the province. Johor has benefited from high levels of investment from Singapore and other East Asian countries. Singapore's rapid economic growth and development as an important international transportation and communication hub have spilt over to Johor, which is becoming an important growth centre for Southern Malaysia, as it gets closey interlinked to domestic economic advantages.[14]

Table Two shows export and import figures between IMS-GT countries from 1999 to 2009. It can be inferred that there has been a considerable growth in trade between IMS-GT members. The fall of import and export figures in 2009 could be an effect of economic recession during this period. It can also be inferred that the formation of the sub-regional trading zone has helped augment economic activity amongst member countries significantly.

Map Four: Map of SIJORI Growth Triangle

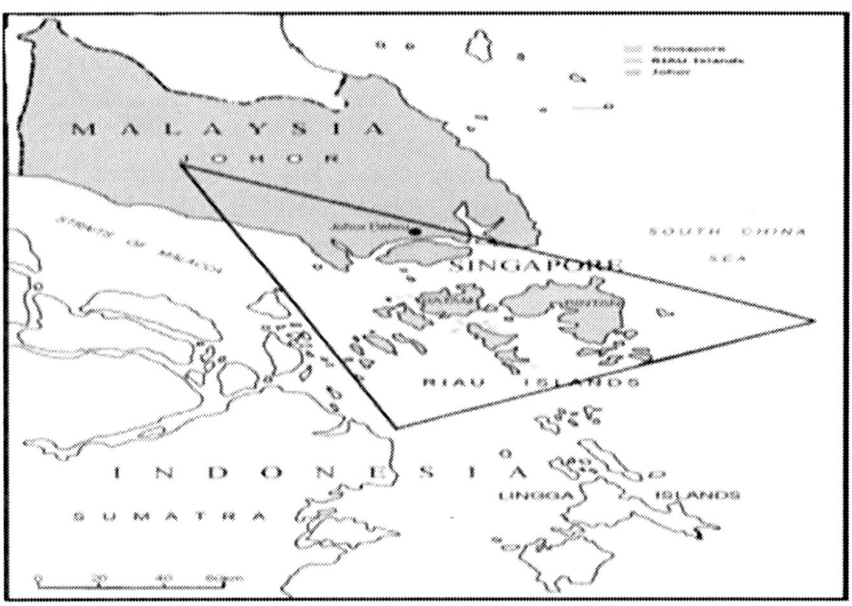

Source: www.iboro.ac.uk

Table Four: Export and Import between IMS-GT Countries (Million)

Trading Group	*Trade Type*	*1999*	*2004*	*2009*
Malaysia-Singapore	Exports (RM)	53,106	72176	77195
	Imports (RM	34,817	44477	48115
Malaysia-Indonesia	Exports (RM)	4,679	11677	17235
	Imports (RM)	6,677	15936	23019
Indonesia-Singapore	Exports US$	4,930	6,001	9,654
	Import US$	2,525	6,082	15,550

*RM denotes Malaysian Ringgit.

Sources: Ministry of Finance Malaysia (http://www.treasury.gov.my) and Statistics Indonesia, The Republic Indonesia (http://www.bps.go.id)

2.5 Southern China Growth Triangle (SCT)

SCT is an association between three regional provinces of China, Taiwan and Hong Kong. It is probably one of the oldest economic integration formations in East Asia. This affiliation was formed to connect Taiwan and Hong Kong with the PRC. To develop the South Eastern coastal regions of China, namely, Guangdong and Fujian provinces, links were established with Taiwan and Hong Kong economic areas. As all the three provinces possessed some form of strategic economic advantage, combining their synergies thus resulted in resolving many of their economic challenges.[15]

Taiwan is considered as a giant in technology and manufacturing from which China has benefitted immensely. China provided Taiwan with cheap labour along with financial support to set up information technology-based industries in the strategic provinces of Guangdong and Fujian. This alliance led to reduction in China's soaring problem of unemployment of skilled youth and also helped develop economically backward provinces. Hong Kong has been regarded as an behemoth trading region in East Asia. The well developed ports, manufacturing, financial services sector with favourable trading policies etc. have all driven phenomenal growth in this region. Hong Kong became a very prominent export destination and has gained vastly from its offshore trading activities. The well-managed financial services industry also shared its expertise and opened financial services centres and branches in the region.[16]

By establishing this triangle, Taiwan gained through access to markets for its manufactured goods, as China is Taiwan's largest import and export partner. China, on the other hand, was able to resolve its problem of unemployment and underdevelopment in these two provinces by importing the industrial base. Hong Kong rendered seamless support to the supply of goods to other parts of the world by both China and Taiwan.[17]

The table below shows the trade figure for SCT member countries from 1995 to 2012.

Table Five: Trade Data of Southern China Growth Triangle Member Countries US$ (Billions)

Trading Group	*1995*	*2005*	*2012*
Taiwan-China	3.4	63.74	121.62
Taiwan-Hong Kong	27.94	36.14	40.59
China-Hong Kong	NA	265.98	341.49

Source: Ministry of Commerce People's Republic of China (http://english.mofcom.gov.cn) and Bureau of Foreign Trade—Trade Statistics, Taiwan (http://www.trade.gov.tw/English).

Map Five: Map of Southern China Growth Triangle

Source: http://www.komagan.com

Each of these brief case studies show that sub-regional cooperation has acted as a powerful tool in addressing the predicament of underdevelopment of depressed regions. The question is how the proposed BCIM growth quadrangle is going to benefit its constituent partners. This is analysed in the next section.

3.1 Bangladesh's Take from BCIM

Bangladesh shares international borders with India and Myanmar. Its geographic location makes it an important participant in the BCIM growth quadrangle. The economy of Bangladesh is largely dependent on agriculture and services sector. Both these sectors together contribute over 80 percent to the country's GDP. Although Bangladesh is rich in land and labour resources, it suffers from capital scarcity, and BCIM could act as an amplifier in this regard.[18] Since Bangladesh has already emerged as a hub for low value-added apparel products, this sector can be vertically integrated with its counterparts in India and China. Infusion of modern technology from these two neighbouring countries can add more teeth to the apparel industry, leading to the enhancement of its competitiveness in the global market.

BCIM is likely to help Bangladesh in leveraging its geo-economic advantage to the fullest. Perched between two natural resource-rich regions—Myanmar and India's North East—Bangladesh will be in a better position to derive economic benefit by way of providing market access and developing resource-industry linkages, which would energise the dynamics of growth across the borders. A synchronisation of natural resources of Myanmar and North East India, market and cheap labour of Bangladesh, capital, technology and managerial skills from China and mainland India can make the BCIM another success story.

Like Myanmar, Bangladesh also has the potential to emerge as a transport corridor for both India and China. If Bangladesh provides transit facilities to India, Bhutan, Nepal, Western Myanmar and South West region of China, it could earn a hefty amount by way of transit fee. Moreover, Bangladesh can also make use of its rich coastline to its advantage by way of providing access to its ports to the neighbouring land locked regions. This will not only revolutionise the structure of internal multi-modal connectivity but also make trade and commerce more competitive. The integration of multi-modal transport network within BCIM would also facilitate the access of Bangladesh to the markets of East Asian countries through Myanmar.

Besides economic benefits, BCIM would also enhance the strategic advantage of Bangladesh as it engages both India and China through this platform. Instead of depending on one country extensively, Bangladesh's strategic space will be widened while dealing with both the regional powers.

3.2 China's Take from BCIM

China looks more at strategic gains from this grouping than mere economic gains. Its interest in this growth matrix is multi-angled and is beyond those of mere immediate gains. Long term politico-economic interests are paramount considerations for the Chinese push to this growth quadrangle. The proposed economic corridor—alongside the "Southern Silk Route"—will liberalise its landlocked Yunnan Province by linking it with the far off Indian market (Kunming to Kolkata), which India has been hesitating to offer ostensibly on security grounds.[19] Located at the South West frontier of China, Yunnan shares boundaries with Laos, Myanmar and Vietnam in the West and Thailand, Cambodia, Bangladesh and India in the South. The proposed integration will help one of the least developed provinces of China to become a platform in its economic engagement with the South Western markets across the border. In addition, the integration of Yunnan with Bay of Bengal as a result of this initiative will, by and large, complement China's trade oriented effort in the neighbouring nations of Bangladesh and Myanmar. Needless to say, this also goes together with China's much cherished 'Two Ocean' strategy.[20]

BCIM will give China access to both Indian markets as well as its resources. A billion plus population with a growing per capita income is definitely of interest to any country. Considering the highly efficient and low cost of production advantage, Yunnan can put up a stiff fight for Indian companies. In addition to this, access to key resources like energy, coal, water, etc. would support the growth trajectory of China. Given the fact that India is China's one of the most important trading partners, the present trade statistics are highly skewed in favour of China, with a trade deficit in 2014 was US$ 37 billion for India. Integrating with India will enable China to facilitate the goal of these two nations to scale up trade even further (expected to touch US$ 100 billion by 2015).[21] The availability of a massive pool of young working population (130 million surplus workers by 2025) in India can be taken by China as a counter to face the challenge of surging labour costs for it.[22] Lest we forget China's eye on the Information Technology sector, that happens to be the most crucial catalyst of India's stunning growth journey over the past decades. Cooperation with India in the field of IT, outsourcing, banking will not only help China to benefit from the latter's splendid expertise in these domains, but also will simultaneously shift India away from making China's contention for power in the Atlantic region intellectually and technologically more sound.[23]

Apart from India, Bangladesh's strategic geographical proximity to the world's most important markets via maritime routes is perhaps the biggest interest for China. It has already gained support of Bangladesh for constructing a rail line between Kunming and the strategically important port of Chittagong in Bangladesh, via Yangon in Myanmar. In fact, China has already started the project of building a container port facility at Chittagong for extensive naval and commercial access.[24] Moreover, the vast unskilled cheap labour of this tiny country makes it a sensible option to locate or relocate industrial units in Bangladesh to attain decisive cost advantage. As far as trade is concerned, the size of trade between China and Bangladesh touched US$ 8 billion in 2012, and China figures as the largest source of imports for Bangladesh.[25] The linking of China with Bangladesh through BCIM has the potential to bring exponential increment by reducing the cost and time of transport between Yunnan and Bangladesh.

China's interest in Myanmar is multi-dimensional. Of the BCIM countries, China shares the closest relationship with this underdeveloped nation, particularly when Myanmar is under self-imposed isolation. Myanmar's enormous natural resource base, especially of natural gas and hydropower, coupled with an extremely strategic geographical location at the junction of South Asia, Southeast Asia and China not only is a source of comprehensive development but also a captive power multiplier for China. It offers the landlocked provinces of China—namely Yunnan and Sichuan—a trading outlet to the Indian Ocean. China is not only the most important trading partner of Myanmar but also the most dominant investor as well. Bilateral trade between these two nations touched US$ 3.6 billion, with investment from China touching as high as US$ 1946.75 million.[26]

Map Six: Map of Kolkata-Kunming Road

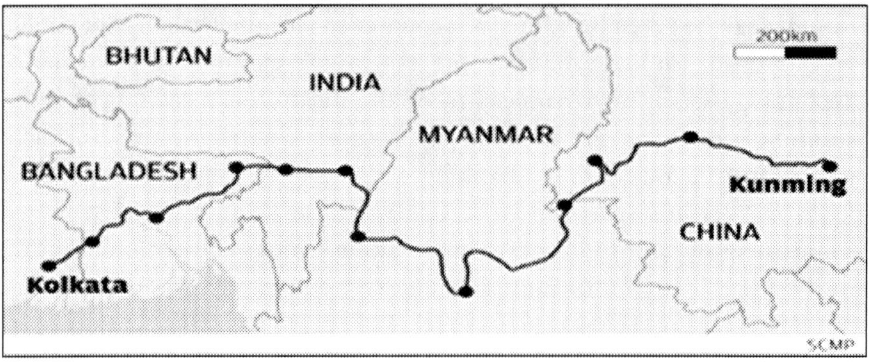

Source: www.scmp.com

3.3 India's Take from BCIM

Unlike China, India so far does not have any success story in the realm of regional cooperation. Neither SAARC nor BIMSTEC could succeed as a model for regional/sub-regional cooperation. Although the LEP has met with considerable success in terms of creating trade opportunities with the countries of Southeast Asia, gains from this policy have mainly accrued to states in mainland India, and lesser opportunities for the border states in India's North East, which suffer from stifling barriers to development due to their remote location and weak links to national market centres. As the principal aim of any strategy on regional cooperation across international borders is to address underdevelopment of the border regions by way of mobilising cross-border synergies, which is otherwise an uphill task to accomplish within national models of growth. This aim has not been fulfilled as far as India's North East is concerned. The proposed BCIM provides an opportunity for India to fulfil this goal.

The BCIM has the potential to integrate India's East and NER with the other three partnering countries over various converging advantages. The 1250 mile-long proposed economic corridor joining Kolkata with Kunming is seen as a road to success for all the four countries involved in this zone. Once Kolkata, Dhaka, Guwahati, Mandalay, and Kunming are interconnected, this is expected to generate strong economic forces to propel growth within the zone. Development of connectivity and multi-modal transportation facilities across the border would enable NER to access markets of neighbouring countries, which in turn would strengthen resource-industry linkages leading to the growth of resource-based industries, as the region is blessed with abundant bounty of nature. Thus, BCIM can be instrumental in addressing the problems of underdevelopment of NER, which otherwise would be a difficult task to accomplish within the framework of national development since market forces tend to bypass geographically peripheral areas.

Besides the interest in development of the NER region, BCIM provides a platform where India and China can work together to uplift the underdeveloped regions lying between them. It will provide a common platform to both the Governments to interact with each other for mutual benefit. It will also increase people-to-people contact between their citizens facilitating better understanding of each other's point-of-view, thus facilitating ironing out the trust deficit and expand areas of mutual cooperation. While BCIM will enable China to have access to the Indian Ocean by way of connectivity in the North-South direction, it would also benefit India by way of facilitating overland access to Southeast Asian countries. Both India and China will be able to enter each other's sphere of influence, leading to increase in mutual interdependence. This will, in turn, expand the space for cooperation and reduce areas of conflict between them.

3.4 Myanmar's Take from BCIM

Myanmar is counted amongst one of the most underdeveloped countries in the world, regardless of being a veritable store house of natural resources like gas. The BCIM economic cooperation will immensely benefit Myanmar in improving its socio-economic stature. It will support its unexploited agriculture sector, assist in energy resource exploration, construction of power plants, building transport infrastructure and create an investment climate for economic development. The agriculture and agro-based processing industry provide major livelihood and employment opportunities for the nation. Through BCIM, Myanmar could gain by improving its agro industries by leveraging the expertise and experience of member countries like India and China. Myanmar is a large exporter of numerous agricultural items like rice and pulses, which member countries are also equally competent in producing and exporting.[27] The forum would provide support in transferring technology which could be used by local producers and farmers in increasing their production so they can meet domestic and international demand effectively.

Myanmar is rich in natural resources like minerals, iron ore, oil and gas. The export of these resources is mostly unprocessed i.e. adding no value to these resources. Thus, the forum will help rope in resource processing units which may act as economic impetus agent for the region and serve as an cost efficient proposition for all member countries in acquiring these resources. This may resolve issues of energy demand for member and neighbouring countries of Myanmar.

In geographic terms, Myanmar is strategically situated. It shares borders with India and Bangladesh on its West and China, Laos and Thailand on the East. This allows Myanmar to be the centre of several transit corridors for other Southeast and South Asian countries. The transport corridor would invite colossal investment from both India and China in building multi-modal connectivity, which can become vital for infrastructure development in Myanmar.[28] Myanmar's long coast line offers immense opportunity to developing sea-borne trade. The construction of ports will connect Myanmar to other destinations of the world. This sea coast advantage can facilitate trade and provide cost effective access to all BCIM members for trading with other nations.

Besides economic advantage, BCIM will also expand strategic options for Myanmar. It can come out of the shadow of regional power(s) and play off both to expand its strategic space.

4 BCIM and the Dividend for India's North East

Like China's South West, India's NER also suffers from the peripheral syndrome. Before the partition of the Indian subcontinent in 1947, NER was linked with the Indian mainland through present-day Bangladesh. The multimodal communication channels between NER and mainland India used to run through the Bangladesh plains. Following partition, these traditional channels of communication were disrupted, making NER a land-locked territory. In post-partition India, NER is connected with mainland India through the narrow "Chicken's Neck", which has widened the geographical distance between NER and the Eastern entry port of India, i.e. Kolkata, at least by four fold. Although NER is rich in resources like hydrocarbons, forests, hydro-electricity and other minerals, high transportation costs did not allow it to grow according to the comparative advantages. The connectivity bottlenecks have made the region perpetually underdeveloped and, hence, politically volatile.

Although NER was supposed to act as the bridgehead to LEP since it shares land border with Myanmar (an ASEAN member country), this role could not be realised since trade between India and ASEAN countries is conducted via sea, thereby benefiting coastal states while the landlocked NER continued to languish in underdevelopment. As it has already been mentioned, both state-led development processes pursued by India before liberalisation and market-led development processes after liberalisation have failed to energise enough growth in NER owing to meagre public sector investment in the first case, and private sector investment in the second, leaving the region largely out of the ambit of of the overall growth drivers of the national economy.

BCIM can provide NER an opportunity to show case its geo-economic advantages—besides strategic geo-political importance—by way of establishing cross-border connectivity and enhancing access to markets of neighbouring countries, making both production and marketing cost effective. Thus, sub-regional cooperation would likely to prove more effective in the development of NER, rather than accomplishing the same through the overall drivers of national growth. Besides economic advantages, BCIM can facilitate a partnership between neighbouring countries and NER. This might facilitate the resolution of conflict in territorial interests in some parts of NER by different players across the borders. And the Indian state may be able to leverage sub-regional cooperation to reign in different non-state actors who are fomenting militancy from the soil of neighbouring countries.

Conclusion

BCIM sub-regional cooperation has the potential to promote growth in South West China, Bangladesh, Myanmar and North East India by way of leveraging complementarities of these regions with each other. China can provide manufacturing inputs, India can provide services, and natural resources from NER, Myanmar can provide natural resources, and Bangladesh can provide the cheap labour. The mobilisation of these cross-border synergies is destined to make BCIM as an economically vibrant zone that can transform the landlocked NER and South West China through the development of cross-border connectivity. The sooner this growth quadrangle comes into being, the better it is for all constituent partners as it puts everyone in a win-win situation.

NOTES

1. Pradeep Srivastava and Utsav Kumar. "Introduction" in Pradeep Srivastava and Utsav Kumar (ed.) *Trade and Trade Facilitation in the Greater Mekong Subregion* (Philippines: Asian Development Bank, 2012), p. 3.
2. Ibid., p. 11.
3. The Greater Mekong Sub-region Economic Cooperation Program Strategic Framework 2012-2022. (Philippines: Asian Development Bank, 2011).
4. Srivastava, Pradeep & Kumar, Utsav, op. cit, p. 3.
5. The Greater Mekong Sub-region Economic Cooperation Program Strategic Framework 2012-2022. op. cit.
6. Ibid., p. 15.
7. Expanding Horizons: A Study on the Development of the Indonesia, Malaysia, Thailand Growth-Triangle Economic Connectivity Corridors (2010).
8. IMT-GT & ADB, "Building a Dynamic Future: A Roadmap for Development 2007-2011", (Philippines: INDONESIA – MALAYSIA – THAILAND GROWTH TRIANGLE, 2007).
9. Emma White. "Tumen River: The Greater Tumen Initiative" (lecture, April 15, 2010)
10. Chung Mo Koo. "Strategic Review on Greater Tumen Initiative", *Tunmen Programme Initiative,* September 19, 2011, http://tumenprogramme.org/UploadFiles/pdf/Strategic%20review%20report%202011.pdf.
11. Chung Mo Koo, Hyun-Hoon Lee and Donna Yoo. "North East Asian Economic Cooperation: Assessment and Prospects of the Greater Tumen Initiative" (Working paper, Asia-Pacific Cooperation Academy Kangwon National University, Chuncheon, Korea, 2011).
12. Anne Marie Humphries. "Growth Triangles of South East Asia" (East Asia Analytical Unit, 1995), p. 29-49.
13. Masahiro Kawai. "Financing Development Cooperation in North East Asia" (working paper, Asian Development Bank Institute, Tokyo, Japan, 2013).
14. Elliot R. Field. "Thinking Outside the Triangle: Collusion and Rivalry between Transnational Corporations and the State in Batam, Indonesia" (Master's thesis, the Centre for International Studies of Ohio University, 2006), p. 13.
15. Aynul Hasan. "Conceptual Framework for Growth Triangles",*The Pakistan Development Review*, vol. 38, no. 4 Part II (1999), pp. 805–822.
16. Shaun Breslin. "Decentralisation, Golabalisation and the Creation of Trans-National Economic Regions in the People's Republic of China" (working paper, Centre for the Study of Globalisation and Regionalisation (CSGR), University of Warwick, Coventry, United-Kingdom, 1999).
17. Jean-joseph Boillot and Nicolas Michelon. "The South China Triangle and Taiwan From a Maquilladoras Zone to an Integrated Economy", *French Centre for Contemporary Research,* (August, 2000), http://www.cefc.com.hk/pccpa.php?aid=1644.
18. M. Shahidul Islam. "China's Look South Policy and Bangladesh's Look East Policy: Convergences and Constraints" (Presented at a seminar on "China's Look South and Bangladesh's Look East Policy: Convergences and Constraints" for the Institute of Governance Studies of Brac University in The Daily Star Centre, October 9, 2013).
19. Debashish Roy Chowdhury. "Southern Silk Road' Linking China and India Seen as Key to Boosting Ties", South China Morning Post, October 23, 2013.
20. Sumedh Lokhande. "India-China Relations: Potentials of Cooperation and Dissonance", *The Wordpress (blog), Chaurahha.wordpress.com,* March 13, 2013, http://

chaurahha.wordpress.com/2013/03/30/india-china-relations-potentials-of-cooperation-and-dissonance/.

21. Yu Lintao. "Reaching Out Across the Himalayas," *Beijing Review*, May 30, 2013, p. 13.
22. Ibid., p. 13
23. Ibid., p. 13
24. Robert D Kaplan. China's Two Ocean Strategy. (Washington, D.C.: Center for a New American Security, 2009).
25. Dan Steinbock. "Bangladesh plays key role in China's Rebalancing in Southeast Asia," *South China Morning Post*, November 4, 2013.
26. Isabel Hilton. *China in Myanmar: Implications for the Future*. (Norway: The Norwegian Peace Building Resource Centre, 2013).
27. Debapriya Bhattacharya and Mashfique Ibne Akbar. "Recent Developments in Myanmar and New Opportunities for Sub-Regional Cooperation: A Bangladesh Perspective" (working paper, Centre for Policy Dialogue, Dhaka, Bangladesh, 2012).
28. Jabin T. Jacob. "The India-Myanmar Borderlands: Guns, Blankets and Bird Flu" (working paper, Cahier de Spirit, 2010).

BCIM-EC: PERSPECTIVE FROM THE NORTH EAST

5

Sub-Regional Initiatives and North East India

T.T. Haokip

Background

The paper attempts to argue that development in India and other sub-regional groupings which are likely to affect India's North Eastern states, should not be based on merely state-centric security outlook but must make the North East an integral component of any initiative. However, lack of proper infrastructure, connectivity and governance make it difficult for the Indian government to incorporate the North East in India's trade expansion strategy with neighbouring countries. While the general perception is that the North East is an important component of India's LEP, BIMSTEC and BCIM, critics argue that the importance of North East for India is confined to acting as a bridge between the India and the Southeast Asian countries. In view of such apprehensions, steps should be taken to ensure that the quest for economic development and integration with other countries does not adversely affect the traditional ways of life of the people of the region and destroy the eco-system in the process. If the problems and apprehensions of the people of the region are adequately addressed, the North East—because of its geographic and strategic location—can emerge as the main trading zone of India. Given its natural resources and strategic location, North East India has the potential to become India's "powerhouse" and a "base" for growing economic links with neighbouring countries in trade and investment.

During colonial rule, the North Eastern states were treated differently from other regions of British India. In a way, even after independence, the North East was neglected for a long time. Largely alienated from the Indian mainstream, North East India has been until very recently considered a neglected and forgotten region of India. Even today, entry to Arunachal Pradesh, Mizoram and Nagaland is possible only through Inner Line Permits (ILP) even for Indian citizens, leave alone foreigners. Of late, the people of Manipur and Meghalaya,[1] too, wanted the same regulation to be made applicable to their states. Interestingly, Manipur, [2] which is a non-tribal state—also complains about the influx of migrants. ILP gives a sense of security to the people of North East India who suffer from the fear that unchecked influx of migrants would pose a threat to their rights, culture and identity. The unabated influx of illegal migrants from Bangladesh threatens to upset the demographic balance of North Eastern states. Tripura and Assam are frequently cited as examples of adverse effects of this influx. These fears cannot be discounted, since Tripura stands out as a classic case of tribals being reduced to a minority in their own homeland. Indeed, influx has affected the demographic, economic and political scenario of Tripura to such an extent that the tribal people are no longer able to determine their own future. Thus, the fear of influx adversely affecting their demographic, economic and political balance has driven the people of North East India to search for possible solutions to their problems through violent or non-violent movements or struggles. Many civil society groups affirmed that the demand for ILP is an integral part of the indigenous people's quest for ethnic identity, and assertion of their right to self-determination. The agitation for ILP very often turned against not only foreign immigrants but also against other migrants from India. The demand for ILP in different parts of North East India has gained momentum because there is a sense of insecurity amongst the people. The real issue is the large scale influx of non-tribals from other states, and not necessarily just foreign nationals. The solution to the problem lies in removing the sense of fear and insecurity amongst the tribal people.

Significantly, a marked feature of North East India is the problem of integration and a history of having the longest-running insurgency in the world.

The strategic location of the region is emphasised by the fact that about 98 per cent of the region's borders form India's international boundaries; it shares borders with China (1100 km) in the North, Bangladesh (4031 km) in the Southwest, Bhutan (410 km) in the Northwest, and Myanmar (1643 km), in the East. Further, the entire area is connected to the Indian mainland by a 22-km land corridor through Siliguri in the state of West Bengal, popularly known as "Chicken's neck". The region is, therefore, more connected to China, Bangladesh, Bhutan and Myanmar than the rest of India. Thus, the centrality of North East India is critical in effectively pursuing economic initiatives with neighbouring countries in South and Southeast Asia. India has immense geo-strategic and security concerns in North East India. Multiple insurgencies in the region survive on smuggling, drug trafficking, gun running and tacit or direct support from the Burmese Junta, China, Pakistan, Bhutan and Bangladesh. Vast amount of arms of American, Russian or Chinese origin have found their way into insurgent hands in North East India, mainly through Laos, Cambodia and Thailand, either through the sea route (Cox Bazaar in Bangladesh) or through the land routes in Myanmar. North East India has become the immediate as well as a long-term challenge in India's overall vision of a new world order based more on trade and less on wars and conflicts. Political instability, ethnic alienation and development lags of the region are, thus, sought to be addressed within the larger framework of India's LEP and other sub-regional initiatives.

Development Dilemma

Notwithstanding its abundant natural resource and liberal funding from the Central Government, the North Eastern region has been deficient on most indices of economic and social development. The North Eastern states continue to decelerate even after receiving special economic packages ever since 1996. Even after more than 60 years of independence, the economy of the region is characterised by a stagnant primary sector, a miniscule industrial sector and a bloated tertiary sector, and the gap between the North East and the rest of India continues to grow.[4] The North East Vision 2020 prepared by North Eastern Council (NEC) documents the backwardness of the region vis-à-vis the rest of the country. Surprisingly, its per capita income had fallen to 27 percent below the national average by 1980, and had further declined to 46.38 per cent below the national average by 2008. In 1999-2000, only Mizoram had real per capita income a little above the national average per capita income (1.3 percent). In 2007-08, states of the region except Sikkim recorded a gap in per capita income as compared to national average in the range of 12 percent for Tripura to 37 percent for Assam. Sikkim recorded a slightly higher (0.8 percent) per capita income than the national average. The Planning Commission Report shows an increase in poverty levels in Nagaland (12.1 percent), Manipur (9.2 percent), Assam (3.5 percent) and Meghalaya (1.0 percent) over the five years from 2004-05 to 2009-10, whereas poverty levels in the country as a whole have declined by an average 7.3 percent.[5] Financially, North East India is in a dismal condition with regard to locally generated revenues in order to sustain a decent living. The Union Government contributes nearly 35, 000 crore every year for a population of 40 million. About 85 percent of Arunachal Pradesh's funds are given by the Centre, Assam has a share of 51 per cent of Central funds; Manipur 80 per cent; Meghalaya 70 per cent; Nagaland 80 per cent, Sikkim 40 per cent; Tripura 72 per cent and Mizoram 70 per cent.

The establishment of NEC was indeed a significant institutional innovation in view of the interdependence of the seven North East economies. However, it is argued that NEC was designed to serve security interests more than to promote integrated development of the North East. This is clear from the fact that NEC was placed for long under the administrative control of the Ministry of Home Affairs, and under the chairmanship of one of the Governors of the region. NEC is conceived as vested with a 'Planning' role—a sort of planning for the NER. In practice, it is a forum under the control of the Government of India for balancing the conflicting claims of the North Eastern states against each other. With the rising importance of the NER, the Government of India set up a separate Ministry for the Development of North Eastern Region (DoNER) in September 2001. The Government of India put into effect a policy of earmarking at least 10 percent of planned budgets of various central ministries or departments for the development of the North Eastern states. The sluggish development and alienation of the region from the rest of the country is a complex and multi-faceted phenomenon, with historical, political, economic and structural causes.[6]

What is surprising is that the region is still plagued with chronic problems of underdevelopment even after large sums of money have been pumped into the region in the name of development. Several proposed developmental packages have been left largely unimplemented because of poor monitoring, lack of accountability and non-adherence to the stipulated time frame for project implementation. What needs urgent attention are proper utilisation of funds and not just the announcement of developmental packages. Some even believe that pumping in money without proper streamlining and utilisation has opium-like effects. The main reasons why pumping funds into the region by the Centre has not had the desired impact include leakage of funds at various levels of the government machinery, funds earmarked for development making their way into the coffers of insurgent groups and lack of capacity in the states to absorb the huge quantity of funds in the absence of expertise to successfully come up with implementable projects and the infrastructure to get some of these projects off the drawing board. Thus, on the development front, North East India has failed to develop its potential largely because of the vicious cycle of political instability, lack of appropriate development and ethnic isolation, besides incessant insurgency and ad-hoc Government policies.[7]

Sub-regional Initiatives

As a part of the endeavour to strengthen India's linkages with East and Southeast Asia and to reinforce the LEP, India has been a part of several regional and sub-regional initiatives over the past few years. These include South Asia Sub-regional Economic Cooperation (SASEC); Mekong-Ganga Cooperation (MGC); BIMSTEC and BCIM.

Look East policy

It may be argued that the policy was crafted originally as a response to the vacuum created in Indian foreign policy, with the sudden demise of the USSR, so as to integrate with the other nations on the Eastern side. The bulk of increase in trade has been shipped through traditional maritime routes. The regions that have gained prominence are the hinterlands of Chennai, Vizag and Kolkata ports in the East. The LEP has yielded many benefits and supported India's economic transformation and growth, including closer contacts between India and Southeast Asian countries, a remarkable leap in the quantum of bilateral trade and increased people-to-people interaction. With outward looking policies, India's foreign trade, which was below US$ 40 billion in the early 1990s, had risen to US$ 140 billion by 2003. Foreign trade as a ratio of Indian GDP had risen from 12 percent in early nineties to more than 23 percent by 2003, pointing to increasing openness of the economy. There has also been substantial progress in India's trade with other developing countries and with Asia, with the initiation of the LEP. The share of developing counties has doubled to about 30 percent of India's trade, while Asia's share has doubled to 24.2 percent.[8] This impressive expansion of trade with India's Eastern neighbours has had little or no impact on the economy of the North East, as this trade expansion has taken place mainly through seaports.

It was only in 2003 that LEP envisaged the region as the centre of a thriving and integrated economic space.[9] Taking into account its economic potential, the policy correctly identified North East India as the gateway to the East and Southeast Asia. A vision for North East India is absolutely necessary simply because there was none in the past. The policy envisages development of the North East Region through increased trade and investment, and by engaging the people of the region in productive and profitable activities. However, when we consider existing ground realities, the growth of border trade between the North East Region and neighbouring countries is slow. Barring the opening of border trade between India and Myanmar at Moreh and Champhai, and between India and China at Nathula, and the much-hyped 165-km long Indo-Myanmar Friendship Road connecting Tamu and Kalaymyo-Kalewa, nothing significant has happened on the ground. Thus, the possibility of North East India serving as the entreport for the entire hinterland of India is likely to be delayed by several decades. Till now, India's policy of developing ties with its Eastern neighbours has been limited to counter insurgency efforts, where the LEP is being used as a means to drive out 'insurgents' taking shelter in neighboring countries like Bhutan and Myanmar.[10]

Role of the North Eastern states in the LEP is in sharp contrast with the role that the Yunnan province plays in China's pursuit of closer ties with its neighbours. There is much talked about opening of new trade routes or reviving the ancient silk route through North East, leading to economic development of the region. Before meaningful trading activities can take place, the region needs to prepare itself, beginning from agriculture productivity. Processing industries have to be set up to manufacture quality agricultural produce which can be sold in international markets at acceptable prices. The entire infrastructure of roads, railways, communication and air transport will have to be completely revamped. Similarly, hotels, restaurants and resorts will have to be built for tourists.[11] If this cannot be achieved, the LEP will not be able to yield benefits to the region and, in that case, it will only act as a corridor between mainland India and Southeast Asia. The North East will gain from FTAs only when there is considerable investment in infrastructure, transport and communication facilities.[12] Thus, the LEP needs a reorientation to suit the development interests of the North Eastern region. LEP only provides a bridge between the rest of India and other countries. According to Atul Sarma, Government of India's hesitation to project North East in its LEP can be traced to five factors:[13] security architecture,militant armed struggle, Chinese expansionism in Southeast Asia, supply of drugs and narcotics, and emphasis on maritime trade and not on land routes. These factors give a comprehensive account of India's restricted attention to the North East as a region to connect with economies of South and Southeast Asia. The success of the policy depends on the commitment of the Government of India to implement proposed plans and projects under the policy and to give a role to the North Eastern states in this policy.

Kunming Initiative

The 'Kunming Initiative' was floated in 1999 and rechristened as the BCIM Forum for Regional Cooperation in 2011 comprises Bangladesh, China, India and Myanmar. The main focus of discussion at the BCIM forum over the years has been connectivity, expressed primarily in terms of trade, transport and tourism, and supplemented by ideas on social, cultural and academic cooperation. The Forum advocates for equality and mutual benefit, sustainable development, comparative advantage, the adoption of international standards and infrastructure development. It talks of realising potential benefits accruing from abundant natural, human and other resources, based on mutual complementarities, through deeper integration of the constituent economies of the BCIM sub-region. It calls for the integration of geographically contiguous and strategically located sub-regions of North Eastern states of India, Bangladesh, Myanmar and South West of China in trade, investment, energy, transport and tourism. Although many dismiss the BCIM as little more than a 'talk shop' not accompanied by concrete activity, its potential cannot be altogether ignored.

The BCIM, with a geographical area of 208,000 sq. km, is a unique forum in many respects. It is one of the very few regional forums in which China and India are more or less equal co-partners, although some Indian observers see it as another Chinese geo-political design to penetrate South Asia. India and China are the two 'biggies' of the BCIM region, and their cooperation is the glue that holds the regional initiative together. While

China and India have comparatively better technology, a more efficient labour force and improved physical and commercial infrastructure, Bangladesh and Myanmar have a large unskilled and semi-skilled labour force as well as basic and intermediate technology. Bangladesh, the most densely populated country in the BCIM, shares a 4,055 and 193-km long border with India and Myanmar, respectively. Bangladesh is surrounded largely by India on all sides except for a small border with Myanmar. It has boundaries with the Indian states of West Bengal and Meghalaya on the North, West Bengal on the West, Tripura, Assam and Myanmar on the East and Bay of Bengal on the West. The natural resource base of Bangladesh constitutes natural gas, arable land, timber, coal, etc. China, the most populous and largest country within the forum, shares 2,185 and approximately 4,000 kilometer border with Myanmar and India, respectively. India shares a border with Myanmar. Yunnan is a landlocked province in Southwest China, sharing 4,060 km long international border with Myanmar. It has been a historically underdeveloped and geographically isolated area. It is one of China's gateways to Southeast Asian and South Asian countries. Yunnan is in many ways similar to North East India. In addition to bringing in lots of benefits, the outward looking development strategy of the region may also import a few vices such as erosion of social bonds in tribal society, emergence of economic inequality, spread of HIV, drug addiction, human trafficking, etc. The economic benefits of the market-oriented, trade-led, outward looking economic strategy would definitely outweigh the real or imaginary cost that we may have to pay. The globalisation process and India's 'LEP can accelerate trade/border trade between India and the Southeast Asian countries, which can bring in progress and prosperity for the entire country. With the developments discussed above, North East Region—with its geostrategic advantage—could emerge as a business transit centre for the BCIM, SAARC and ASEAN groups of nations. A major impediment in the growth of border trade with India's Eastern neighbours is the absence of a strong and efficient transport and communication network between India and the countries of BCIM. To derive benefit from border trade, physical linkages amongst trading partners in the form of trans-national highways, railways, waterways and airways, wherever possible, are essential. A huge amount of capital expenditure would be necessary to build such facilities, which is possible only through financial assistance from international financial institutions and investments by multinational corporations (MNCs).

The issue of connectivity and development of trade linkages can be further augmented by exploring how physical connectivity can help reduce input costs of production and help trade between countries of India's Southeast. Given the centrality of linkages through North East India, road and air linkages will help strategic hubs of trade and commerce in the region. In this way, one can imaginatively think about trading possibilities across Stilwell road that would connect Ledo with Myitkyina in Myanmar and onto Kunming in China. The whole road can be utilised not only for transporting goods, but also for providing necessary linkages for developing ancillary industries. Such linkages between ancillary and main industries can help these areas develop into major manufacturing hubs in North East India. Indian exports can move to Yunnan, and then to Rangoon in Myanmar to Bangkok to Singapore, to cover the whole physical spread of a possible trading zone.

The larger issue that needs to be delved into is to what extent this infrastructure connectivity can be sustained by trade, commerce and industry. Developing indigenous industries in North East India is beset with hurdles. Starting with relucatnce of banks to offer attractive loans and capital, one also shudders at the only option of developing natural resource based industries that deplete nature and pollutes the fragile environment of the North East Region. A well-articulated development plan must have a component of connecting the South Asian road building initiative with initiatives for industrial productivity and growth, basing them in the North East Region. LEP or initiatives like BCIM still lack this critical component of linking connectivity with industry. As a result, the North East, being a backward region industrially and economically, will only become a corridor. This corridorisation of the region will bring greater disharmony between the State and the market. Thus, the framework of a well-articulated policy for connectivity and development will require sustainable augmentation of local resources and local economic participation.

Another critical issue that needs to be looked into is the impact of resource extraction on the cultural and ecological situation of North East India. Culturally, most communities of the region depend on rice for their livelihood and hence, there is a critical need for conserving bio-resources such as water and forests for sustaining these communities. The capital-intensive model of industrialisation does not take into account culturally rooted and nurtured lifestyles and worldview of the people of the North East and hence, there could be the possibility of irreconcilable conflict with the cultural moorings of the region. How these cultural groups and communities survive on their own and develop a production surplus is still a matter of concern. If one fails to take into consideration the lived reality of peoples and communities of the region, capital intensive plan for industrialisation only displaces these communities from their ethnic style of living and substitutes existing modes of production of the region by something that remains parasitic on the resources of the region, while at the same time fails to deliver employment or enhance production.

The current BCIM initiative cannot limit itself only to building a 16-lakh sq km road, but needs to go beyond by strengthening the local economy from within. Mere plans of investment on infrastructure and trading between countries only would not help the North East. Even generation of power and exchange of energy resources will need industries that consume these energy resources. Else, carrying gas, coal, petroleum and other such resources from and through North East will only create a super-rich elite trading to the detriment of the traditional agrarian economy. It makes little sense to encourage fly-by-night operators whose only mission is to set up profitable industries and extract natural resources by diverting investments from core industries to natural resource sector, as it happened in various countries across the world. This is predictably clear, as has happened in many regions of the world, that capital-intensive industries located in these areas to increase their profits and ended up by extracting only the natural resources of these regions.

There is a need to emphasise on regenerating bio-resource based agriculture and other related cultivation practices to replenish the rural, tribal and ethnic economy of the region. An initiative such as BCIM can benefit more people by taking into account the livelihoods of the peoples of North East and Myanmar, if not in Yunnan and Northern Thailand. Augmenting bio-resource dependent livelihoods of the hills, forests and riverine sub-regions of the BCIM will sustain the initiative in a more meaningful way. Especially, agricultural livelihoods like rice cultivation, animal rearing and fishing should receive significant attention, something that capital intensive industry tends to overlook. Investments that are at cross-purposes with augmentation and strengthening of local livelihoods will bring in a kind of neo-colonial grabbing of prime resources from communities to private parties, who only appropriate resources without any resultant building up of capacity. In order to ensure the well-being of the peoples of NER, any inter-governmental initiative must take into account each other's weak spots and initiate a move that addresses these, and then goes on to strengthen the local economy with its close association to livelihoods, ecology and culture.

It is necessary to understand that peoples and communities not only want development but also want respect for their identity. Given the in-built suspicion and conflict over many a trifle issue such as land, river or boundary, a resolution of such inter-state rivalry and dispute should be a pre-requisite before proceeding with any model for international co-operation. In the context of BCIM, such inter-sate rivalry creates distrust in establishing people-to-people contact, as they are restricted by international boundaries. The proposed BCIM has to allow non-military travel and people-to-people exchanges on their own terms, and not by means of monitoring and surveillance by states. This could be a tall order, given the existing local ethnic struggles for greater share of power and resources. At the same time, it is necessary to realise that while security issues are important, opportunities to conduct business in free and fair environment are necessary preconditions for growth of the NER and other regions of India. Will BCIM states come out of this security-centric approach and join the process of people-centric development?

NOTES

1. For details on ILP in Meghalaya, See, H. Srikanth, C. J. Thomas and Recordius Enmi Kharbani. *Vision for Meghalaya On and Beyond the Inner Line Permit* (Guwahati: ICSSR-NER 2014), pp .1-111.
2. The Government of India Vide Letter no.120/47/C-26-27 dated 17th January had officially approved retention of the permit system in Manipur in 1948 but abolished by the then Chief Commissioner in 1950.
3. T.T. Haokip. "Kuki Armed opposition Movement", *Eastern Quarterly*, vol. 6, no.1&2 (2010). p.16.
4. Kishan S. Rana and Patricia Uberoi. *India's North East States, Monograph: The BCIM Forum and regional Integration,* Institute of Chinese Studies, Delhi, vol.1. December 2012, p. 34.
5. For more details, please see, http://planningcommission.nic.in/news/press_pov1903.
6. Rana, Kishan S. and Uberoi, Patricia, op. cit, p. 21-24.
7. Prasenjit Biswas. "Post-Development, democratic Discourse and Dissensus: A Critique of vision 2020", *Eastern Quarterly,* vol. 6. no. 111&1V (2008), pp. 178-188.
8. Sushil Khanna. "Economic Opportunities or Continuing Stagnation" Gateway to the East: a symposium on North East India and the Look East Policy, *Seminar*, June 2005.
9. Rajiv Sikri's lecture 'North East India and India's Look East Policy', in CENISEAS Forum 'Towards a New Asia: Transnationalism and North East India' held at Guwahati on September 10-11.2004
10. Sushil Khanna, "Look East, Look South: Backward Border Regions in India and China", www.burmalibrary.org/docs4/LookEast-LookSouth-08REVISED.pdf.

11. H.N. Das. "Preparing the North-East for Look East Policy", *Dialogue*, vol. 9, no. 1, July-September 2007.
12. T. Haokip. "India's Look East Policy", *Third Concept—An International Journal of Ideas*, vol. 24. no. 291 (2011) pp. 7-11.
13. Atul Sarma, "North East as Gateway to Southeast Asia: Big Dream and Home truths" Revised version of Presidential address delivered at the Seventh annual Conference3 of the North Eastern Economic Association held at Rajiv Gandhi(arunachal) university, Rono Hills October 21-22, 2006.

6

BCIM-EC and the North East: Explaining India's Reluctance

Binoda Kumar Mishra

The idea of BCIM originated in 1999 from Kunming since the Kunming Initiative is yet to achieve anything substantive. It is widely believed that it is India that is the reluctant partner in the arrangement. In an era of regional cooperation, India's reluctance is inexplicable to many analysts in India and abroad. The paper would make an attempt to explain this so-called reluctance. It proposes to argue that North East India is the reason for India's go-slow approach to BCIM. The nature of the proposed BCIM arrangement and the economic disparities that exist in the BCIM region are unlikely to produce equal economic dividends for all members in the arrangement. In a gain calculation, India perceives itself to be the least gainer from the arrangement, given the present economy of the NER. No matter how sound the economic arguments are, interstate regional arrangements are always subject to non-economic strategic calculations.

Added to this, the North East is extremely volatile with a web of issues, identity, development, migration, demography, etc. Some of these issues have serious security implications. Thus, in an environment where in Indian Foreign Policy is constantly under scrutiny of the strategic community, changing the nature of engagement with some neighbours, particularly China, is not easy. Appropriate preparedness is required to make use of the economic opportunities India's neighbourhood offers, while guarding its strategic interests and concerns. There is a need for a clear economic plan along with economic preparedness and strategic hedging. While economic preparedness and calculations must be North East-centric, strategic hedging would remain predicated on the emerging larger regional security architecture.

In this context, the paper will seek to suggest that an incremental approach, based on pragmatic cooperation at the *provincial and sub-regional level,*[1] is the most effective option. Cooperation within the BCIM context, but on a much smaller scale, must be promoted in a planned way, leading to preparedness of the North East to benefit from the proposed BCIM-EC, akin to the EU. Stakeholders from the region should be facilitated to interact amongst themselves to work out mutuality of interests and promote people-to-people contact for sustained engagement, till the North East is ready in all respects to benefit from the BCIM-EC arrangement in an equitable manner.

Who Proposed the BCIM Idea?

In pursuance of the proposal of the Chinese Premier, Li Keqiang, on October 23, 2013, in a joint statement, both the former Prime Minister of India and the Premier of China declared their intent to explore possibilities of establishing an economic corridor comprising South-western China (Yunnan Province), Myanmar, Bangladesh and North Eastern and Eastern parts of India. The Joint Statement proposed to constitute a joint study group for this purpose. The study group has met once in Kunming in December 2013 and produced a roadmap by December 2014. Though these are seemingly positive developments, there remains great doubt over the idea finally materialising in the near future. Thus, the pertinent question is why such doubts have been expressed at the highest political level between the two most important partners to the arrangement? To get at the answer, one has to interrogate the BCIM idea in detail. The main aspects that need interrogation are: who proposed it; why was it proposed; who will benefit and how much; who is most reluctant and why, and, finally what are India's options?

The BCIM was launched as the Kunming Initiative, a Track II sub-regional initiative, in 1999, to promote sub-regional economic integration of Bangladesh, North East India, Myanmar and Southwest province of China

(Yunnan). The basic premise was to re-integrate regions that were integrated economically and culturally a few centuries ago. The Initiative intended to address structural impediments to the development of the region. It aimed at making borders irrelevant, increase connectivity and facilitating economic development on the principle of mutual economic complementarity. The broad rationale of the initiative was to create conditions for the overall development of the region by providing the region access to sea—applicable to Southwest China and North East India—and to provide opportunities to Bangladesh and Myanmar to gain from their engagement with bigger economies like India and China. The economic logic was sound, and there was an equally sound reason for China to initiate this arrangement. From mid-1990s, China has implemented a deliberate strategy of opening up its border provinces (selectively) for transnational economic interaction. Yunnan has been one such region that has been allowed to interact with the economies of Southeast and South Asia. In Chinese policy terms, Yunnan is termed as the "Bridgehead" for China with South and Southeast Asia.

Yunnan is already connected to many ASEAN countries, and is fast emerging as a trade hub between China and the mainland ASEAN countries. There is demonstrated success of this policy for Yunnan's economy, as it claims to be developing at 12.1 percent annually[2]. One can wonder as to what specific benefits China wishes to gain from the BCIM arrangement for its Yunnan province. The general logic given is providing Yunnan sea access. Yunnan's present engagement with ASEAN countries, particularly with Myanmar, does not provide sea access to Yunnan, thus making the logic of leveraging sea access seem weak as a motivation for BCIM. The second reason advanced is access to the Indian market. This can be a plausible logic, but considering that the original BCIM idea takes only North East India into consideration—which is not an improved market—the logic of accessing the Indian market within the BCIM region is not strong, and only makes sense if the whole of India is taken as a part of the BCIM arrangement. It can certainly be argued that the Chinese strategy does include the whole of India and the whole of China, as the scope of BCIM increases in future. The declared Chinese objective in favour of BCIM, however, is to promote development of the region in line with the Chinese strategy of "peaceful rise" and "friendly neighbourhood".

The BCIM idea continued at the Track II level for a considerable period of time, starting from 1999. In a sense, it has not yet been elevated to the Track I level as the Chinese tend to believe that just because the term "BCIM" figured in the joint declaration of both the Premiers during their meeting in October 2013 is not significant by itself. While the Chinese have lent full Governmental support to the arrangement from the very beginning, the Indian side has been the most reluctant, as is made out to be. Myanmar and Bangladesh, the other two players in the arrangement, seem to welcome the BCIM idea. The idea was acceptable to everyone in principle so long as there was no progress on the ground, but since both China and India are now planning to put the idea into action, serious calculations have begun in all the four countries—and more particularly in India—as it has been the most reluctant player in the arrangement. This brings us to the point where we need to have a detailed discussion of the intent of the protagonist of the arrangement, China. The PRC, after liberalising its economy in 1979, experienced rapid economic growth to the extent of replacing Japan as the second largest economy in the world. But development in China has not been uniform, and there exist severe disparities amongst provinces. Broadly, coastal Chinese provinces have experienced rapid industrialisation in comparison to the Western hinterland provinces. These provinces—such as Yunnan, Tibet and Xinjiang—lagged considerably behind the developed Eastern provinces in terms of economic progress that China experienced. This necessitated introspection on the part of the Chinese leadership to find reasons for the relative underdevelopment of these provinces, and ways to improve the economic scenario in these underdeveloped provinces.

Among the reasons that were floated to explain the relative underdevelopment of the Western provinces was their landlocked character, poor resource base and lack of access to immediate markets. In order to overcome these shortcomings and to put these provinces on the path of rapid growth, the Chinese Government realised the need to grant some amount of autonomy to these provinces to interact with countries in their immediate neighbourhood, who could either provide access to sea, augment accessible resource base and provide a market for products produced in Yunnan. Emerging Southeast Asia was seen as an opportunity, so was also the geographically contiguous South Asia. Yunnan, thus, was granted relative autonomy—as compared to other provinces—to engage with its geographical neighbours. Yunnan quickly took advantage of its geographical location and turned itself into a gateway for China to the ASEAN region. ASEAN engagement is providing Yunnan with growth opportunities which have resulted in a growth rate of 11 percent, compared to the national growth rate of 7.4 percent.[3]

Encouraged by such growth—and realising the need for sustenance of such growth—Yunnan wishes to expand the scope of the regional engagement beyond its current level with ASEAN countries. India emerges as a potential partner for long-term economic prosperity for its South Western region. If one looks at the initial articulation of the BCIM idea, it talks about inclusion of the North Eastern part of India in the arrangement. This shows how Yunnan has rationalised the economic engagement with NE India on geo-economic similarity. The rationale often provided for economic integration of the proposed region is to increase economic growth in this relatively underdeveloped region through mutual cooperation. It is a sound argument for sub-regional cooperation amongst four countries, that otherwise experience underdevelopment due to lack of either resources, markets, technology and finance or connectivity within the region and to the outside world through ports. But the next question is who would gain the most from such an arrangement, since we know that in international relations, economic gains are not always calculated in absolute terms. More often than not, they are calculated in relative terms, particularly so when the involved partners—especially the dominant ones—are pitted in a competitive rather than cooperative mode. In this case, India and China are not the countries that would calculate their pay offs from any arrangement in absolute terms given their juxtaposition in the emerging international order, the baggage of history, and the almost irresolvable border dispute. These apart, both have the compulsion of ensuring resource security for their billion plus and still growing populations. Their own resource requirements will force them to face each other for resources. Thus, competitiveness in India-China calculations in the current and future calculus, is genuine. The question that becomes significant, thus, is 'who gains more?'

Between India and China: Absolute Gain is Relative Loss

The question of gains—relative or absolute—arises only when we are willing to cooperate. Therefore, the first question that comes to mind is—does India have any reason at all to be a part of an arrangement involving China? Added to this are anxieties related to the risks of opening up of NER for cross-border interface. India's NER is economically stagnated and needs to be opened to the external world to improve the economic situation. In the present era of globalisation and trends in reaping benefits from regional economic arrangements, India certainly can think of regional arrangements that benefit its NER, particularly when all other domestic endeavours have failed to lead to economic development in the North East. Actually, the idea of economic development of North East through economic engagement does find place in India's LEP, even though as an afterthought. Though there is a lot of rhetoric about the NER benefitting from the LEP, nothing has actually materialised on the ground. Arguably, this is because of the problem of choosing whether it should be security first or development first. This is rather avoiding the issue. The primary reason for NER's below par development after independence is the secluded nature of the region—economically, politically and socially.

The current geo-economic space in NER does not have the dynamics to unleash development from within and sustain it. Questions of identity that have bothered India since independence were instrumental in India having an economic and cultural hands-off approach towards NER. This, in the words of Jairam Ramesh, was the first of the "paradigms" of the "paradigmatic" approach of India towards the North East.[4] A "culture paradigm", sensitive to the distinctiveness of the culture of the NER, induced India to allow the region to operate on its own terms not only culturally but also economically. Interaction with Indians from other parts was limited. This was expected to provide the NER the space to manage its economic, political and social fabric in its own terms and not feel the pressure of imposition of a completely different economic and social model. Enjoying economic and cultural liberty, it was assumed that the people of NER would assimilate into the Indian political union. The result was just the opposite. Moderate economic development in the rest of India and its absence in NER escalated the sense of alienation in the NER. Wide-spread resentment was the political fallout of this sense of relative deprivation. Parts of the region even attempted at secession from India. The Indian approach towards NER changed under this volatile security scenario, and the culture paradigm gave way to a "security paradigm". The region saw increasing use of force by the Indian Union without matching or compensating economic benefit. Insurgency could certainly be contained to a large extent, but its elimination has not been possible till date. Secondly, the involvement of insurgents in economic activities parallel to the legitimate economy, and their unofficial writ over large parts of NER, is crippling the "development approach" the Government of India has embarked on in the NER. The reason is again lack of economic dynamism within the region, preventing NER from taking off economically.

The potential of NER's cross-border interaction leading to economic development was the only rationale for including it in the LEP, but its failure in yielding results varies from the mere presence of insurgents and the resultant insecurity. The major economies of Southeast Asia are better connected to India through the sea and find no compulsion to interact with the NER economy directly. Countries like Singapore, Malaysia and Thailand would prefer sea trade and commerce to that of taking the overland route through the NER. The only economy of Southeast Asia that is connected with NERis Myanmar. BIMSTEC could have supplemented the LEP had it taken off by now. But for various reasons, BIMSTEC is yet to take off. Central to NER's deprivation in LEP and BIMSTEC is lack of connectivity to a larger economy, developed and complementary to NER's economic potential. China (Yunnan to begin with) presents NER with that opportunity. But the trouble is India cannot completely trust China, and particularly so when it comes to its underbelly, i.e. the NER. Even if there are clear indications that NER may benefit from engagement with a bigger economic neighbour like China, India is still unsure about the prospects of BCIM. The reasons are varied and valid.

The Concerns

Security concerns apart, the economic rationale in favour of engagement may turn into a concern if, as proposed or expected, BCIM-EC materialises today and the region is economically made an integrated one. Then the question is—who will benefit more? An evaluation of the preparedness (economic) of BCIM region shows that China stands at the top. Owing to its already (relatively) developed economy, manufacturing expertise, improved infrastructure, stable political system and a controlled wage structure, Yunnan will offer itself as the natural destination for any industrial investment, depending on the resources of the region. Parts of BCIM other than Yunnan naturally would then end up as mere industrial peripheries, just supplying natural resources and helping Yunnan to develop as an industrial giant. It has been often alleged that resource-rich areas have seldom benefitted, at least immediately. This happened during the not-so-past colonial era, and is still happening at the national level as well. If one notices, the map of resource-rich India and poor India are very distinct even today. Therefore, the onslaught of the Chinese economy on NER has to be avoided under any circumstances.

The second concern is about uncertainties prevalent in and around the region. For example, in Myanmar, one cannot be sure of domestic developments in the country. There are currently invisible but serious implications of Myanmar's domestic issues—particularly the issue of ethnic harmony—for India and its engagement with Myanmar within BCIM. The unstable political arrangements between the Central Government and the various ethnic groups based on agreed ceasefire(s), leave most parts of the Myanmar border under de facto writ of the ethnic groups, some of whom are certainly well armed. It only adds to India's concerns that some of these ethnic groups provide shelter to major Indian insurgent groups, both for economic reasons and for primordial affinities. No corridor between India and China involving NER can escape the influence of these armed groups. If the sovereign writ of the Myanmar Government is so limited, one has reason to doubt it will improve in the near future, particularly when there is no sign of a rapprochement amongst the ethnic communities themselves.

India has begun to face up to the implications of ethnic disharmony in Myanmar. The Rohingyas, who are a minority community of Muslims, are not acceptable to Myanmar. They are being severely persecuted there. Recently, the Rohingya issue in Myanmar had has its repercussion in India. India now wakes up daily to the possibility of half a million displaced Rohingyas from Myanmar and Bangladesh heading towards India. There are already over a thousand Rohingyas in India. While there is sympathy for homeless people everywhere, one cannot be oblivious to the possibility of this stateless population, taken care by none and bearing no allegiance to any nation-state which can be used to cause internal problems in India. In India, the Rohingya connection to the Bodh Gaya explosions has not been completely written off. The bleak prospect of a harmonious ethnic arrangement in Myanmar, wherein Rohingyas are accommodated, and the unwillingness on the part of Bangladesh to entertain them, does not promise anything better, either for the Rohingyas or for India.

Third, the issue has direct implications for the security concerns of India. Continuous seizure of Chinese-made arms indicates the existence of an well-oiled network of underground (non-state) actors in the region. The story of smuggled arms reaching NER is not old. Developments like the Wa (called the Speed Tribe) State Army actively manufacturing and circulating legitimate or illegitimate Chinese guns along with lethal methamphetamines, has serious consequences. For instance, the first manifestation of the consequences of illegitimate Methamphetamines is the threat of extinction to the traditional opium consuming Shangpo tribe of Arunachal Pradesh.

Even economically, dealing with Myanmar is more a concern than an opportunity. The border trade agreement between India and Myanmar was signed in January 1994, and implemented in April, 1995, with the opening of a cross border point between Moreh (Manipur, India) and Tamu (Sagaing Division, Myanmar). The volume of trade through this pass looked encouraging initially, but it slowed down later. In 1996-97, the volume of border trade amounted to Rupees 31 crore of Indian exports of and Rupees 15 crore as imports. This figure declined to Rupees 5 crore in exports and imports by 2004-5.[5] This is in contrast to the overall increase in bilateral trade between the two countries. The possible reasons for such decline in the official volume of border trade can be the presence of insurgents on both sides of the border, and, more importantly, insurgents taking over trading activities and running a parallel trade arrangement in both legal and illegal items. Whatever may be the reason, the net result is that border trade is not helping the local community for whom it was primarily initiated. Rather, it is contributing to strengthening the insurgent groups. It can be argued that with development of the local economy, there would be enough to lure the insurgents to abjure their current occupation. But at this point in time, the risk is more than the benefit.

India's Options

The easiest of the various options for India is to avoid any engagement that has China as a member—and an important one. This can be rationalised on the security pretext, as there are numerous security concerns—both traditional and non-traditional—in engagement with China that BCIM offers. We need to ask: will this help India and NER in anyway. As already pointed out, China can provide the much-needed ignition to the NER economy and avoiding engagement with China will close this opportunity for the NER. This is not to argue that NER cannot develop at all without engaging with the Chinese economy. LEP and BIMSTEC can bring in development to NER, but slowly, in a trickle-down effect—through Myanmar in case of LEP, and Bangladesh, Bhutan and Nepal in the case of BIMSTEC. Availing the Chinese economic opportunity will boost the NER economy and, supplemented by LEP and BIMSTEC, the NER can experience a faster pace of growth much needed by the region. If India feels there is benefit in engaging China—which are in fact there are—can one devise a way to engage with China that negates the concerns such an engagement may bring.

The way out is exercising the option of engagement with China in a calibrated manner. The first doubt often expressed is that in the event of economic integration, goods from China would flood the markets of India's North East. This, at best, is a symptomatic manifestation of the real fear. There is no study available to calculate the relative payoffs to China and India from economic arrangements under BCIM, but the present advantage China has over India in terms of preparedness in reaping economic opportunities is jittery enough for India and it apprehends that in the event of economic integration of the region, total control of the regional economy would possibly be in Chinese hands. Thus, while it is advisable to protect NER from the economic onslaught of the Chinese economy, limited economic interaction between NER and Yunnan should be allowed, based on the potential of the NER economy. In overall calculation, the NER economy may look weaker vis-à-vis the Chinese or Yunnan economy, but close scrutiny shows there are some sectors in which the NER enjoys relative advantage. The NER states must be invited to join the India-China engagement from their positions of strength and need. These are sectors wherein NER can negotiate from a position of strength.

Only way India can bring about economic growth in NER is by providing it with real opportunities of showcasing its advantages in tourism, handicraft, horticulture, non-timber forest produce, etc. Of late, without any Government intervention, healthcare services in parts of NER are proving to be a success. The talent of NER youth in IT sector is well acknowledged. Based on these advantages that India (NER) has vis-à-vis China, India can initiate the process of limited economic engagement with China and, subsequently, expand the scope to include other sectors in the arrangement. For example, during the 9th meeting of the K2K Forum[6] held in November 2013 in Kolkata, the state of Tripura expressed its desire for access to Chinese technology in the bamboo sector and market access for bamboo products from India, which it believed could contribute tremendously to the economy of Tripura. Similar optimism is seen in other NER states vis-a-vis engaging with China. Based on such advantages, if the NER is gradually allowed to be involved in the India-China bilateral and, subsequently, BCIM-level economic interaction, the dormant economy of NER would gain some momentum. If this dynamism leads to economic revitalisation, other economic activities can be included to expand engagement. An economic rationale thus can be built in the not-so-distant future to invest further in infrastructure and improve connectivity within NER, and expand it within the region.

The limited engagement will protect the underprepared NER from losing out to China in all-out competition in its current state of economic preparedness. At the same time, the NER can benefit from the opportunities of Chinese market and technology to harness its economic potential. Since interactions will be limited and graduated in nature, the progress will be easy to monitor, and India retains the flexibility and scope to arrest or reverse any negative spill over that might emerge due to intended or unintended actions of China and/or itself. Positive spill over can be used as a building block for slowly expanding the scope of engagement, both with China and with other BCIM partners, to other sectors based on the NER' strengths. This definitely sounds easier said than done. But there is no harm in trying this out, at least for a short period of time. In fact, whatever little engagement that has occurred within the recent bilateral goodwill gestures has proven that there is a lot of enthusiasm not only within NER, but also in other provincial economies of India, such as West Bengal, Bihar and Odisha. The K2K Forum that operates as the only civilian bilateral initiative between India and China that facilitates provincial (sub-regional) level economic, cultural and academic exchanges, has succeeded in demonstrating the success of sectoral cooperation between Yunnan and West Bengal in various sectors. Such experiments must be encouraged and emulated at the regional level. Based on the demonstrated success, business stakeholders from NER, backed by political will of North Eastern States, are joining the K2K process. The success of these stakeholders must be closely studied and the positives be carried forward into other sectors. When such incremental engagement covers most sectors of the economy of NER, the idea of an BCIM Economic Corridor is complete.

The benefits of engaging China through BCIM must not be judged in terms of its positive impact on the volatile security scenario in NER. Creating scope for developing legal stakes in the NER economy for its population can be expected to be both an incentive and compulsion for the economy and, it is expected, leading to reduction in insurgency. Concerns vis-à-vis China, either in strategic matters or on pending bilateral issues, are not going to disappear soon. Even if BCIM leads to success, India must not be complacent about Chinese intensions. There should not be any laxity in strategic and military preparedness to meet exigencies against the Chinese. Finally, there remains one practical hurdle for any form of operationalisation of BCIM-EC. So long as the BCIM economic idea is on the drawing board, one can avoid the issue of Arunachal Pradesh by drawing the corridor on the physical map; but when it is operationalised, Arunachal Pradesh cannot be kept out of the zone. This will raise a very sensitive issue with a fairly rapid potential for escalation of tensions between India and China. The final advice, thus, to both India and China would be to realise that since they have lived with the reality (status-quo) for over six decades, there is no harm in engaging each other based on the status-quo.

NOTES

1. As spelt out by Former Indian Prime Minister Dr. Manmohan Singh during his October 2013 visit to Beijing.
2. Brian Eyler. "A Quick Glance at Yunnan's 2013 GDP," *East by Southeast*, February 3, 2014, http://www.eastbysoutheast.com/quick-glance-at-yunnans-2013-gdp/.
3. This year the Chinese economy is growing at 7.4 percent as reported for the first quarter of 2014. See, Keith Bradsher. "Growth Rose 7.4 percemt in First Quarter, *China Reports*," *The New York Times*, April 15, 2014. The current growth rate of Yunnan is claimed to be 11 percent as claimed by the Governor of Yunnan during an interaction with this author on March 28, 2014 at Raj Bhawan, West Bengal.
4. Jairam Ramesh talks about Indian Government adopting a paradigmatic approach towards NER, such as 'Culture Paradigm', 'Security Paradigm' and 'Development Paradigm'. For detail, see, Jairam Ramesh, "North East India in a new Asia," *Seminar*, 2005, http://www.india-seminar.com/2005/550/550%20jairam%20ramesh.htm.
5. C.S. Kuppuswami, "Indo-Myanmar Relations-A Review," Paper No. 2043, *South Asia Analysis Group*, November 30, 2006, p.3.
6. The K2K Forum (Kolkata to Kunming) Forum originating in 2002, is the only civilian initiative between India and China at the provincial level. The Forum facilitates sector specific economic, cultural and academic engagements between Southwest of China and Eastern provinces of India. The 9th meeting of the K2K Forum was held in Kolkata during November 21-22, 2013. Around 50 delegates from various economic sectors along with academics and political representatives participated from China. From India, apart from West Bengal those states that sent political representatives or officials are Manipur, Assam, Bihar and Tripura. For details see, www.csird.org.in

BCIM-EC: CHALLENGES AND PROSPECTS

7

BCIM-Economic Corridor and India-China Relations

Ravi Bhoothalingam

Introduction

India and China are the world's second-largest and third-largest economies, respectively.[1] Their combined population is one-third of the globe. Yet, engagement between their economies remains modest at best and people-to-people contact is minuscule. Will the BCIM-EC be a significant step towards India's comprehensive engagement with China? And will it help the two countries to create win-win solutions to address poverty and develop their border regions in an equitable, balanced and sustainable manner?

In many ways, India and China are polar opposites. But, looking forward, the paper shows how complementarities in capabilities between India and China can unleash innovation and creativity in both countries, addressing common peoples' concerns as well as global problems. The paper suggests a new model for India-China economic and regional cooperation that could also lead to the rejuvenation of economies of countries in our common neighbourhood. This means rethinking concepts about borders and borderlands and looking at investments that benefit all regional actors, rather than a narrow perspective of inclusion or exclusion. Certainly, the ideas stated here will come up against the highly securitised mind-set in India that currently weighs heavily on any initiatives in connection with China. The irony is that the proposals in this paper will enhance, rather than jeopardise, India's security. And India's primary national interest, above all, must be to ensure that its people are prosperous and secure. That requires economic dynamism of an order that is possible only when China-India economic relations stop being constricted by the border issue. The Economic Corridor between the two countries would be an example of one step towards building a wider canvas of engagement between the two countries. Several such steps could lead—ultimately—to a breakthrough in political relations.

Background to the BCIM-Economic Corridor

In 1999, academic institutions from India and Bangladesh, and Governments from Myanmar and the Yunnan Province of China, first came together in Kunming, China, with a view towards setting up a sub-regional forum comprising China's Southwest, India's North East and the two neighbouring nations of Myanmar and Bangladesh. This sub-regional forum, named 'the Kunming Initiative', set for itself the goal of bringing this hitherto backward and relatively under-developed part of Asia into the mainstream of development. The key assumption was that this sub-region of Asia had rich potential in both natural and human resources, which if organised and connected through modern infrastructure and communication, would result in its revitalisation. The result, the narrative proclaimed, would be the modern rejuvenated version of a region that in historic times had prospered by its overland connection through the legendary "Southern Silk Route". There are references in recorded history of people and goods being traded overland from Yunnan to India, on a network of trade routes as early as the second century B.C.

The initiative made slow progress until 2013, when a Kolkata-to-Kunming car rally, sponsored by Indian and Chinese Governments, helped bring to public attention the fact that the region could indeed be linked, which in turn could unlock its vast and hitherto unutilised economic potential. Later the same year, the former Prime Minister of India and the Chinese Premier, at their meeting in New Delhi in May 2013, agreed to consult other countries (Myanmar and Bangladesh) in setting up a joint study group to examine the possibility and implications of a Bangladesh-China-India-Myanmar Economic Corridor (henceforth BCIM-EC). After further discussion, a Joint Study Group of the four countries was constituted and concluded its first meeting, held, most fittingly, in Kunming, on December 19, 2013, where a concrete time-table and action plan was agreed about the next steps ahead. The second meeting of the study group was held in Cox's Bazar, Bangladesh in December 2014.

The beneficial impact that regional connectivity and easier movement across borders will have on livelihoods and incomes of people does not have to be emphasised. Examples abound—the European Union, ASEAN, Mercosur, the Central Asian Customs Union and several others—all uphold this lesson. Yet, India's embrace of the BCIM-EC remains somewhat constrained. This reticence can be traced to two factors, which are in turn inter-related: the first is the 'C' in BCIM (India's 'China Syndrome'), and the second is India's nervousness in exposing its sensitive and troubled North East as the first port of call in a possible new era that might, in time, lead to open borders and free trade. In subsequent sections, this paper examines both these factors in turn.

History and the Shadow of Geopolitics

India and China are two of the world's oldest civilisations that have contributed immensely to each others' artistic, cultural and scientific heritage over the last five millennia. They are both large and populous countries, focused over the last six decades in developing their economies and societies from situations of dire poverty, violence and social unrest. In this task, China has been spectacularly successful, India less so but still with a commendable record. So it is not surprising that in the modern age, they are regarded as two upcoming global powers that are likely to shape the future of the world in many ways.

In historical terms, the rising trajectories of China and India merely represent the restoration of their respective positions[2] two hundred years ago. Yet, this phenomenon causes anxiety amongst those Western powers that have enjoyed dominance in global affairs so far, but who now face the prospect of a changing world order with the rise of a number of nations with growing economic and geopolitical weight. This anxiety is felt more in respect to China than with India, because China's political system is seen as alien and totalitarian and, secondly, since China's outstanding success in its economic and social transformation over the last six decades is seen as a formidable challenge.

This situation is ripe for the spread of Western theories of geopolitics,[3] based on the doctrine of the 'Westphalian' ordering of inter-state relations, wherein two rising powers must necessarily be in contention or else one of them must settle for a subordinate position. These theories would claim that in a world so far dominated by the United States (and now challenged by China), the choice before India is whether to ride with the US (and thus insure against China) or to maintain its independent policy and risk Chinese domination.

For these reasons, there has been a distinct tendency in Western discourse to position India and China as 'natural rivals', and to emphasise their differences rather than their commonalities. There are strong industrial and corporate lobbies which derive advantage from such a stance, the global arms industry being a primary one. And the differences between India and China, undoubtedly, are legion. India and China are very different, if you look at their histories as unified states, their languages, religions or customs. Divided by the mighty Himalayan Mountains, there has been little discourse between them over the last thousand years, though the preceding millennia saw greater connectivity including the spread of Buddhism from India to China. The vast difference between Sanskrit, the root language of the Indic world, and Mandarin, in their linguistic structures are indicative of very different ways of thinking in the two respective cultures.[4]

To these differences can be added more recent aggravations between these two rising giants. Border disputes and other irritants have clouded political relations between India and China, resulting in a short but bitterly-remembered war in 1962. The huge and, until now, rapidly increasing trade relationship between the two countries is skewed and unbalanced in China's favour, as the raw materials which constitute most of India's exports to China are less value-additive than the machinery and project goods India imports from China. Investments in each others' economies are minute, and there is little other connectivity. Indian tourists to China number less than 600,000 per year, whilst Chinese tourists to India are only about 100,000. And no wonder, since for the ordinary Chinese person, Indian visas are not easy to get. These minuscule numbers tell a dismal story, given that both countries have a sizable middle class and a large cohort of outbound global travellers, 50 million for China and 15 million for India.

A little knowledge is a dangerous thing, and adding fuel to the above fires is the reality that India and China are profoundly ignorant about each other. There is only a small core of academics and students studying the languages and culture of the other. The level of intellectual and cultural exchanges is low, given the size and depth of the two countries' cultural heritage. India and China may be considered as rising powers by others, but to each of them, the other is *terra incognita*. The media in both countries hardly features the other country; but when it does, given the nature of all media, it is more than likely that the other country is either exoticised or demonised. As stated earlier, the arms lobby, in particular, and their associated interests would profit by a state of underlying tension in India-China relations. As a result, a safe working conjecture to summarise the current China-India relationship would be that attitudes to China amongst the Indian intelligentsia range from the indifferent to the hostile.[5] To India, China is 'the other'. And to China, India remains a conundrum to those few in that country who care to think about it.

It would, therefore, suit the West eminently if India joined them in a 'China containment' plan, but even if that were not feasible, an India that is uneasy and suspicious about China would still do as a second-best option. But the key question for *us* is: what is it that best serves *our* national interest? It is to this question that we now turn.

What is India's National Interest?

This is a question that has been debated *ad infinitum* and has produced a huge diversity of response, since everyone declaring himself or herself as a patriotic Indian will feel entitled to attempt an answer. So who better to give us a perspective on this question than the former National Security Adviser (and earlier Foreign Secretary) of India, Mr. Shivshankar Menon? In a remarkable speech delivered on the occasion of the Prem Bhatia Memorial Lecture in August 2011[6], he clarified the essence of India's national interest. It is worthwhile reproducing some key lines from his exposition:

> I proceed from the assumption that our primary task now and for the foreseeable future is to transform and improve the life of the unacceptably large number of our compatriots who live in poverty, with disease, hunger and illiteracy as their companions in life. This is our overriding priority, and must be the goal of our internal and external security policies. Our quest is the transformation of India, nothing less and nothing more...

And further:

> India's interest is clearly in an inclusive world order, with China as one of its cooperative members. That is clearly what we need to work towards; along with China itself...But this will require much better communication between India and China, and no misunderstanding of each other's actions and motives. This also requires that some of our media and commentators, whose unquestioned brilliance is regularly on display lambasting other countries for their politics and policies, learn the virtues of moderation. The Chinese cannot believe that these media and commentators do not speak authoritatively for the country, as does their controlled media and academia. We must recognise that other countries, too, could have similar imperatives as ours and their own reasons for what they do. And why create self-fulfilling prophesies of conflict with powerful neighbours like China?

Remarkably, very soon after this speech by Mr. Menon, former Chinese State Councillor, Dai Bingguo (coincidentally Menon's one-time counterpart as Special Representative in the China-India boundary talks), wrote a signed article in the *Daily Telegraph* of London on September 26, 2011[7] , where he articulated China's national interests. What is notable is the congruence of objectives in these two documents.

And, more recently, whilst delivering the Sardar Patel Memorial Lecture on October 15, 2013[8] , Mr. Menon took up the same thread in a different vein, emphasising what the intervening two years have brought out in sharp focus: "it is primarily our internal strength that we must rely on to navigate the complex international system......." Then, expounding further on the theme of the transformation of India as the primary goal, he states: "...engagement with the rest of the world is what we must implement; engaging the world from strength whilst recognising reality for what it is, forswearing hubris and belligerence."

Simply put, these three pieces collectively emphasise that the primary tasks of poverty eradication and of assuring their peoples a life of dignity, health, education and welfare will preoccupy India and China for a long time ahead. Mr. Menon points out that 'internal strength' (which can only emerge from economic and social transformation) is a fundamental prerequisite for success in this venture. His caution on '*hubris and belligerence*', whilst addressed to India, should not be irrelevant to the mandarins in Zhongnanhai. After all, even if the most optimistic growth forecasts for China and India come true, by 2040 China will just about reach, with a lot of luck, 40 percent of the per capita Gross National Product (GNP) of the US. India will still be some way behind. Militarily, the US continues to spend more on defence than the rest of the world put together. The message is very clear. It is highly unlikely that the US will be seriously threatened either politically or militarily by a rising China (or India) in the foreseeable future, and it will still remain the leading global power.

The current India-China relationship, therefore, leaves India in an unenviable place. On the one hand, the prevailing mood of mutual wariness results in low and sub-optimal mutual engagement. When two of the worlds' largest economies fail so spectacularly to interact, their people forfeit the many benefits and multiplier effects that would arise as a result. On the other hand, India is landed with all the costs of added security to face 'the China threat', including that of an arms race which could seriously limit the massive effort that is required for India to lift herself out of poverty and backwardness.

Civilisational Roots for a New India-China Relationship

If the current relationship with China as described above does not serve India's interests, what then is the alternative that will do so? To explore that question, we need to take a step back and re-examine the many differences that distinguish China from India, but from a new viewpoint—that of the civilisational heritages of the two countries. Yes, India and China do differ on all the counts stated earlier, and on many more, and there remain serious points of contention between them. Yet a common and profound philosophical thread runs between the two countries: the belief that differences and variations between peoples are not sources of opposition let alone of enmity. Rather, they represent springboards of creativity that could add value to both cultures. "Harmony is not the same as uniformity" said Confucius, and indeed harmonisation can only take place when diversity is present. India's philosophy and its entire living culture too are celebrations of diversity. Both the concept of *ardhanari* in India and of *yin-yang* in China demonstrate how apparent opposites are essential for novelty and creativity.

Moreover, both civilisations affirm that beneath the surface where contradictions are visible, there exists a deeper layer with consonance and commonality at the level of nature and humanity. Thus, the surface trends are illusions and temporary turbulences, which need to be skilfully managed so that they do not destroy the underlying unity. Mao Zedong put it pithily when he talked about 'the correct handling of contradictions'.[9] So one can argue that, through their very differences, India and China possess the civilisational wherewithal to manage their contradictions and hence to orchestrate their 'rise' to be peaceful and productive. This historical legacy enables the use of ambiguity and fluidity as assets in managing turbulence, cross-currents and apparent contradictions.

Let us retrace a step and go back to the root languages[10] of the Indian and Chinese civilisations, Sanskrit and Mandarin, respectively. These languages could not be more different, in script, grammar, construction and syntax. The highly visual and character-based Chinese language stimulates different areas of the brain compared to the complex, grammatical and alphabetic language that is Sanskrit. Modern neuro-linguistic theory[11] has established that the structure of a language shapes the ways in which their speakers perceive and think about the world. This should not be read as a deterministic rule but as an influencing tendency which, when aggregated over a large number of events, results in India and China displaying noticeably different behaviours.

If we carry this argument forward, we can state[12] that, due to their unique heritages, India and China have each developed a set of capabilities which find themselves handily complementary to each other. Take a well-quoted pair: the much-vaunted abilities of China in manufacturing and India's skills in software and I.T. There are several other 'natural fits': China's infrastructure expertise along with India's management and consulting skills; China's strengths in biological and chemical sciences alongside Indian skills in medicine; China's pedagogy and India's English-language strengths; Chinese choreography and India's cinema (Bollywood); Indian chess and Chinese *weiqi*—the list can go on.

Moreover, many common elements bind India and China together. Both are highly populous countries which are only part of the way on their journey to provide a decent standard of living for their peoples. Even if their economic growth rates continue on their past trajectories for the next twenty years (a highly unlikely prospect), China's per capita GDP would still be less than half of today's US levels, whilst India might reach around one-third. Monumental social, economic and environmental challenges face both countries as they strive to achieve these goals. Many of these challenges, as well as their solutions, are relevant to both countries: water scarcity, sanitation, low-cost housing, solar energy, tropical diseases, female empowerment, minorities and their welfare, etc. Why should each country seek to reinvent the wheel?

The Economic Sinews for a New Relationship

It, therefore, makes eminent sense for India and China to collaborate in all these fields. Imagine the benefits to both countries—and indeed the entire world—if India and China could energise the potentialities inherent in the complementary capabilities listed above. India-China joint research programmes could invent a pollution-free car, a US$ 20 computer, a US$ 1000 home, vaccines for malaria, dengue and encephalitis, online education for the poor, water-conserving methodologies, world-beating China-India joint-ventures in high technology areas and the frontier sciences, higher agricultural productivity, people-friendly banking and financial instrument.

The benefits of cooperation are not just in the blue-sky arenas of research and development. No country in modern times has elevated itself into the ranks of the developed world unless it has enhanced substantially its participation in international trade. India cannot be an exception. And where can the sources for such an expansion lie? In North America and Japan, the recovery of their economies from the global financial crisis is as yet weak. Europe is still in a parlous condition. China and the emerging markets, which are still growing robustly (though not at the hyper-speed of earlier years), remain the best bet. The rejuvenation of trade between India and China on a new track, and its optimisation, is thus a priority.

The irony is that both countries live with the counterpoints of surpluses and deficits, with no mechanism to match the same. China is awash with surplus capacity in core industries like steel, cement, machinery and fertilizers, whilst India reels under the impact of persistent inflation due to scarcities and shortages caused by supply-chain inadequacies and logistics covering sectors ranging from food items to coal and energy. India also has also a large but unexplored potential to export to China. But there is such a deficit of detailed and granular awareness in India of Chinese markets at the local and provincial level, that a lot of market demand is missed through lack of signalling mechanisms. India and China need to strengthen the eco-systems necessary to facilitate trade, investment and business interaction between each other. These include strong trade and industry councils, legal firms, conflict-resolution mechanisms, credentialing authorities, mutual acceptance and certification of specified educational and trade qualifications, etc.

European and North American companies enjoy this kind of support infrastructure in China, whilst Japan and Korea have the advantage of long historical business connections. ASEAN, indeed, operates a surplus in its trade with China since it has adroitly inserted its intermediate products into China's supply and production chain.

There is a lesson here for India that if it addresses the issues of its production economies aggressively, there can be a substantial reduction in India's current trade deficit with China. As China moves up the value chain, it will vacate spaces that can be taken up by Indian manufacturing industry, as is indeed happening right now with Vietnam and Bangladesh, and in some sectors in India as well. This can escalate the share of manufacturing in India's GDP, with its positive consequences on employment and incomes, as well as the general level of competitiveness of Indian products. More open borders and easier movement of goods will of course give rise to some imbalances, but the much-feared 'swamping' of Indian markets by 'cheap Chinese goods' as contemplated by opponents of the BCIM-EC is likely to be only a localised and short-lived phenomenon.

The immediate issues and problems of both countries can also be the targets to generate common win-win solutions. For example, India has a huge deficit in terms of its physical as well as social infrastructure, roads, bridges, ports and transportation. The investments required are monumental, and India will need a major infusion of foreign funds in addition to its own savings. But who has both the capacity in surplus funds and the motivation to invest in India? China seems the best bet. China has a massive US$ 3 trillion-plus pile of foreign reserves. Its cumulative investments in Africa are now testing the limits of acceptable levels of country risk. In the Western world, Chinese investments face political opposition and non-tariff barriers, or else, as in Europe, they carry large-scale risks. For China, India is a safe investment bet, with its large market size, financial infrastructure and political stability. The match seems perfect, so what is holding it up? The spectre of security risks and cyber-espionage! A more sober appraisal of risk and reward could create an environment for a win-win solution: where Chinese investors receive a reasonable return on their Indian investments, whilst India creates the much-needed physical and social infrastructure along with employment opportunities through the revival of manufacturing industry.

But the benefits of large Chinese investments go further; they can cover the capital account deficit that India runs with China on the trade account.

For China too, Indian industrial and service inputs can contribute to the achievement of its twelfth Five-Year Plan, currently under way. India is one of the world's largest producers of generic drugs, which are rapidly gaining ground all over the world as healthcare costs mount in both the public and private sectors. They can reduce costs significantly for China in her quest for a comprehensive public healthcare system. India's service providers and increasingly Indian industry as its productivity improves and China's costs go up, can cater to the varied requirements of a China turning towards increasing consumption. The interfaces of the world's second and third largest economies cannot but be myriad, once they are given full play.

Another interface is bound to be tourism. China is projected by the World Tourism Organisation to send out over 100 million outbound tourists by 2020. Even with five percent of that number, India will double its present uptake of foreign tourists. Tourism is an industry with a high multiplier effect on secondary and tertiary services. It has the advantage also of a high employment ratio, creating more jobs and livelihoods per unit of investment than agriculture or industry.[13] Tourism also has the flexibility of employing people on a seasonal and/or part-time basis. These formats suit many people like women or students, who may have other responsibilities but who yet need to augment their incomes. And talking of sustainability, the tourism industry has self-interest in being ecologically responsible, since tourists will shun polluted environments and unhealthy or unsafe practices. Most importantly, the people-to-people understanding that will result through increased contact is the best remedy not only for the India-China knowledge gap referred to earlier, but to create the missing and much-needed emotional connection between the two peoples.

India, China and the BCIM: Rejuvenation of the Neighbourhood?

As India and China reconnect under the new paradigm, the region it will affect most will be the common neighbourhood of India and China. Hopefully, both India and China realise that their journey to prosperity cannot succeed if countries in the vicinity remain backward and poor. Moreover, cooperation through a judicious choice of China-India joint projects in the vicinity may be a more efficient strategy rather than relying only on rivalry or exclusivity. This will also wean the neighbours away from a Machiavellian game of playing China and India off against each other, their natural response if one is engaged in the Westphalian contest of 'spheres of influence'. But in this globalised world, no place is anybody's backyard. So it may be useful for India to study how China plans and executes its strategy of economic outreach.

Three strands may be identified in how China approaches its neighbours. The first emphasises the importance given to creating and maintaining a web of infrastructure and physical connectivity to the neighbouring regions. Second, the border is seen as a tool that facilitates interaction across it rather than as a barrier. Third, the simultaneous promotion of tourism and people-related services goes along with hard infrastructure and investment.

All three components are visible in the China-Myanmar case, for example. There is an excellent expressway system across Yunnan to the border town of Ruili, and Chinese-built roads of good quality extend up to Mandalay. Ruili itself is a well-developed city which services a fast-growing hinterland. Chinese oil and gas pipelines are under construction from the Bay of Bengal port at Kyaukphu to reach Yunnan. They will reduce the risk to China, which would otherwise have to ship the oil through the Malacca Strait.

Similar experiences are evident in other border regions. The border towns in Eastern Siberia are bustling and dynamic, though more on the Chinese than on the Russian side. Pipelines carrying oil and gas for China snake across Siberia. There is a similar network of oil and gas transport networks being built from Xinjiang into the 'Stans' of Central Asia. Railway yards and depots are active in Mongolia to move natural resources to destinations in China and to its shipyards for export. The Qinghai-Tibet Railway, which has already been extended to Shigatse, is further planned to be extended from Lhasa to Kathmandu in Nepal during China's thirteenth Five year plan, and a proposal to create 'an economic corridor' is under discussion between Bangladesh, China, India and Myanmar (BCIM). The latest initiative is the 'Maritime Silk Road' linking China with ASEAN and the Pacific. Chinese tourists form the majority of visitors to Mongolia, Korea, Myanmar and ASEAN countries, whose nationals are increasingly frequent visitors to China.

India needs to reflect on its border policy as applicable to its engagement with China or even with ASEAN, and central to this process will be its conception of the borderlands and their role in the national economy and international trade. As the lead player in SAARC, it is India that must take the initiative in creating vibrant links between the SAARC nations. For this, India may have to go the extra mile and examine the calculus of benefits and costs in a different light. Not all pioneering ventures and outreach initiatives by others are necessarily sinister vehicles of encirclement. A new lexicon is needed to elevate the nations of the SAARC sub-region from their current state of under-development and low levels of mutual trust and it is India that must start to write this lexicon.

A policy of positive outreach to India's neighbours means that borders and boundaries need to be re-conceptualised to become enablers rather than obstacles to trade, investment, tourism and ideas. As we do so, we will encounter in our neighbouring countries Chinese, Japanese and third-country ventures also exploring opportunities there. We must actively explore how we can engage with these players. Ideally, what should emerge is a network of relationships which run the entire gamut from competition to partnership. Now the question arises: is it too naïve to think of India-China joint ventures in Myanmar or Nepal? Or opening India's borders to a much greater extent to trade and commerce, which will improve peoples' livelihoods? A 'siege mentality', which fears being 'overrun' by foreign goods, will result in an India that will simply be bypassed in the geo-economic corridors of the future. India is quite competitive in a range of goods and services even now, and can do far better when we put our house in order. Indeed, it is here that we must improve our overall competitiveness in cost and quality, rather than expending our energies in displaying an obsessive fear of 'encirclement'. That will only result in our economic isolation.

The North East and its Role in the BCIM-EC

Contrary to the nervousness expressed in some quarters of India's Central Government, the feeling in the North East about the BCIM-EC appears to be one of cautious optimism. By and large, the North East accepts the rationale of geography that proximity to China and Southeast Asia must be used as an asset rather than a liability. And the key to accomplishing that task is to list out the unique assets and attributes that India's North East has to offer. Here, pride of place will need to be given to the rich diversity that exemplifies the North East, be it in terms of the ethnological and cultural diversity of its peoples or in its variety of biodiversity in landscape, plant and animal life. Therefore, any development strategy that covers the North East needs to be framed to respect these attributes, and to respond with a creative design that not only accommodates—but draws strength—from such unique assets.

Indeed, the North East's apprehensions of the Corridor are more directed towards the extractive exploitation or in the environmental damage that might occur in its name through an inadequately planned exercise. To avoid both of these consequences, it is vital that consultative mechanisms are built in to ensure local consultation and participation in respect of projects in the area. Another reservation pertains to the notion that the BCIM-EC might be 'a strip of tarmac' merely used to transport giant containers from point A to point B, without creating value addition on the way. Again, this requires the planning of proper ancillary roads and financial linkages that can connect local market towns and energise production, exchange and commerce in local communities. The Corridor is, therefore, more a synonym for a comprehensive plan to address the development needs of the North East in a holistic perspective.

Whilst a detailed plan for such development needs to be made out following the report of the Joint Study Group set up under the BCIM-EC rubric, some broad contours can be indicated. Firstly, the natural and human assets of the North East, as spelled out earlier, lend themselves to an imaginative plan to create the area as a unique Asian eco-tourism destination.[14] The Eastern Himalaya, for instance, has a large number of unclimbed peaks, and its rivers and valleys offer great scope for climbing, caving, trekking and hiking. The terrain can support a variety of wild-life and bird-watching tours, as also adventure sports, ethnological and spiritual tourism. There is a global clientele for such offerings. A network of air-strips and light aircraft, cross-country tracks, eco-friendly lodges and modern eco-tourism tradecraft can create the necessary infrastructure to support such an industry that is both employment-generating and in harmony with nature.

Secondly, another source that can generate employment and incomes would be agricultural produce and livestock, forest-based products and floriculture. Thirdly, with a relatively high incidence of English-speaking youth in the region, IT and IT-enabled services could be developed to serve the region. Finally, the environmentally-sensible management of rivers and water resources, particularly with trans-boundary cooperation—could be an example of harmonious development to conserve water resources and also generate energy as well as to control floods in the entire region. This is a notoriously contentious area, and any progress would be exemplary.

Why should all this happen in the North East with BCIM-EC, when it has not done so in the past several decades? There are several reasons to be hopeful. For a start, the region surrounding the North East is no longer as undeveloped as it was once. Infrastructure in Tibet has developed apace, Bhutan is on the march with the new Government in place, and the last two years in Myanmar have seen distinct changes for the better. Secondly, at least two out of the four BCIM countries, China and Myanmar, have experience of the GMS initiative, where six countries at widely differing levels of development have cooperated in common socio-economic and infrastructure projects. Finally, China has suffered some recent reverses in Myanmar (particularly the suspension of the Myitsone Dam project), which must have delivered the lesson that the pursuit of pure economism devoid of any environmental or ethno-cultural sensitivities can boomerang. These experiences collectively should, we hope, feed into an approach towards the BCIM-EC which will be more informed, holistic and inclusive, and thereby accelerate the process of development in the North East.

The New Civilisational Challenge for China and India

Nations, like people, are held back by their histories and their traumas. In these instances, someone in the neighbourhood needs to step up. For East Asia, it was Japan which first took the lead towards modernisation, but the torch did not survive the initial journey and has now passed to China. For South Asia, it must be India. These two most populous countries on earth and its rising powers must create a new pathway for progress. For this to happen, they need to work together with understanding and knowledge of each other, without '*hubris and belligerence*', and demonstrating leadership but not hegemony. No doubt there will be turbulence from time to time which will need mature and skilful management. These are skills the two countries have possessed for centuries, even though the practice might have become rusty of late. As the traditional engines of economic growth in North America and Europe slow down or even falter, it is more incumbent on China, India and the emerging economies not just to fill the gap but to do so in a different way.

All civilisations have grand projects which leave a mark on mankind. What will China and India bequeath the world? The most recent empires, the British and the American, produced great works of infrastructure like the Suez and Panama Canals. Will India, Bangladesh, Myanmar and China have the patience, the perseverance and the vision to exemplify—by their modern recreation of the once-renowned Southern Silk Road—a new way in which countries, large and small, can cooperate to shape human society in peace and harmony? The world awaits the answer.

NOTES

1. International Monetary Fund (2012). Estimates for 2012 of country GDP (Purchasing Power Parity).
2. Angus Maddison. *Statistics on World population, GDP and Per Capita GDP, 1-2008 AD, 2011,* at www.ggdc.net/maddison/oriindex.htm.
3. Significantly, during his visit to China in October 2013, former Prime Minister Manmohan Singh in his address to delegates at the Central Party School Beijing on October 24, 2013 said: "...old theories of alliances and containment are no longer relevant".
4. Ravi, Bhoothalingam. "Ways of Thinking: Psycholinguistic Reflections on Sino-Indian Relationships and Potentialities", *ORF Discourse,* vol. 5, issue 2, Observer Research Foundation, New Delhi.
5. The Pew Global Attitude Survey for Spring 2012 shows negative Indian attitudes to China totaling 31 percent, ranging from a rating of 'Very Unfavourable' to 'Somewhat Unfavourable'. 45 percent gave a 'Don't Know' opinion.
6. Shivshankar Menon. "*India and the Global Scene*", (Prem Bhatia Memorial Lecture, New Delhi August 11, 2011), maritimeindia.org/article/india-and-global-scene.
7. Dai Bingguo, *The Daily Telegraph,* September 26, 2011.
8. Shivshankar Menon. (2013). Available at prasarbharati.gov.in
9. Mao Ze Dong. *On the Correct Handling of Contradictions among the People: Collected Works of Chairman Mao,* (Beijing: Peoples' Publishing House 1957).
10. We take the liberty in the interest of simplicity of terming these as 'root languages' on the basis that about 80 percent of the respective populations has a working familiarity with their root language as a *lingua franca.*
11. Lera Boroditsk. "Linguistic Relativity" in L.Nadel (ed). *Encyclopaedia of Cognitive Science,* (London: MacMillan, 2003).
12. Bhoothalingam, Ravi. *op. cit.* (for the complete argument to arrive at this conclusion).
14. Ravi Bhoothalingam. "China's South-West and India's North-East: Comparisons and Learning", *Administrative Staff College of India Journal of Management,* vol. 37, no. 2, March 2008.

8

BCIM-EC: Promises and Pitfalls

Rahul Mishra

Regionalism and sub-regionalism have become the buzzwords in the world that is defined by interconnectedness and multilayered politico-strategic and economic linkages across the board. In contemporary times, the geopolitical situation has compelled to embark on regional and sub-regional cooperation and set up multilateral groupings to enhance cooperation. Such initiatives are primarily taken by countries that are geographically contiguous. Since the end of the World War II, multilateralism has been increasingly accepted as the *modus operandi* in world politics in general, and global environmental politics, in particular. Over the last few decades, nations have come to realise that the challenges of security, peacekeeping, disease control and human rights violations amongst others, are too enormous and complex for any nation or group of nations, no matter how powerful, to effectively manage on its own.[1] To deal with such threats, regional and sub-regional cooperation is essential.

In this context, it is imperative to understand the true essence of multilateralism, which has emerged as a determinant component of international relations, particularly in the years following the end of the Cold War. For instance, BIMSTEC, MGC and East Asia Summit are some of the examples of multilateral grouping which came into being in the post-Cold War era. Clearly, to minimise the transnational threats and maximise mutual benefit, cross-border regional cooperation has become a prerequisite.

When the Cold War ended, it led to the end of the bipolar world, which gave birth to new trends in international politics such as globalisation and regionalism. These new trends supported the idea that multilateralism are the way forward for countries to maximise diplomatic and economic benefit. Prominent scholars such as Robert O. Koehane define multilateralism as 'a practice of coordinating national policies in groups of three or more states, through ad-hoc arrangements or by means of institutions.'[2] Another scholar, John Ruggie explains that "multilateralism refers to coordinating relations among three or more states in accordance with certain principles".[3]

There are no two views about the fact that the concepts of regionalism and sub-regionalism is gaining prominence in the present world order. This is largely due to the fact that the enduring pursuit of regionalism and sub-regionalism has an underpinning of peace, security and development through exploration, identification and gradual intensification of trade, economic and cultural ties amongst geographically contiguous areas.[4] One may note that regionalism and sub-regionalism are recent phenomena and have gained prominence only in the late twentieth and early twenty-first century. Regionalism refers to a process in which sub-state actors become increasingly powerful and independent of the state: power devolves from the central and state to regional Governments within it.[5] At the international level, regionalism refers to trans-national cooperation to achieve a common goal or resolve a shared problem; also, it symbolises attempts to reinforce links between countries which are linked by geography.[6] It is in this context that sub-regional cooperation amongst geographically contiguous countries is deemed necessary to solve problems of underdevelopment and accomplish mutually agreeable goals. It has been seen that mostly, sub-regional cooperation has taken place amongst countries whose peripheral areas are vulnerable to ethnic unrest and have porous borders with neighbouring states. Conditions like these have made it necessary for countries to cooperate so as to ensure cross-border cooperation for stability. It is not surprising, therefore, that sub-regional cooperation in particular has been most commonly used as a tool to ensure stability and development in the peripheries of many countries. For instance, China has initiated many sub-regional groupings so as to give a fillip to its less-developed provinces. GMS (Greater Mekong Subregion) Economic Cooperation Programme and BCIM (Bangladesh, China, India, Myanmar)—Economic Corridor are cases in point.

It is in the context of increasing importance of sub-regional cooperation in the strategic and economic calculations of countries that this article aims to explain the trajectory of BCIM (Bangladesh-India-China-Myanmar). The focus is on BCIM because of all the regional and sub-regional groupings, this is emerging as one of the most discussed forums. This paper also tries to understand the prospects and pitfalls in the way of the BCIM sub-regional forum.

Background

Almost all peripheries in Asia are populated by discontented ethnic minorities. In addition, most of Asia's borderlands are porous. For instance, China often calls its Asian neighbours "periphery countries" (*zhoubian guojia*). All its frontier regions are dominated by ethnic minorities and unrest plagues almost all its peripheral areas. Prior to the end of the Cold War, although it was always aware of the importance of maintaining stable relations with peripheral countries for national security, Beijing was never able to make an integrated policy towards its neighbours.[7] It was only in the 1990s that China began to realise the importance of engaging its neighbours. That is how China's 'good-neighbourly' policy was reinvented in the 1990s. One may argue that China was motivated by its own interests and calculations; that is how it initiated the process of constructive engagement with peripheral countries. Similar was the case of India. India's NER (North Eastern Region) has always been geographically isolated and poorly connected with other Indian states. In fact, North East India is far closer to Myanmar than New Delhi. Considering the geostrategic location of Myanmar—which is India's gateway to Southeast Asia—it has always been important for India's North East. These geostrategic compulsions, coupled with the disintegration of the USSR, gave birth to India's LEP (Look East Policy) in 1992.

So far as Myanmar is concerned, it chose to cooperate with its two giant neighbours, India and China. For almost half-a-century, Myanmar was under self-imposed isolation and it was only in 2011 that Myanmar emerged out of isolation and embarked on political, democratic, social and economic transition. Nevertheless, prior to these developments, owing to various economic and political sanctions by the West, Myanmar had close relations only with China and, to a lesser extent, with India. As far as Bangladesh is concerned, the consistent political and economic instability, coupled with civil unrest in Bangladesh, have not augured well for the country.

In the 1990s, these four countries were in dire need of boosting their respective economies—mainly Myanmar and Bangladesh—while India also needed to ensure development of its NER. In China's case, the leadership was reinforcing its good neighbourly policy with the aim to open up the borders of its land-locked provinces to neighbouring countries. The idea of having a sub-regional grouping amongst Bangladesh, China, India and Myanmar was first mooted in 1999 in Kunming, the capital city of China's southernmost province, Yunnan. This was termed as 'Kunming Initiative' in 1999, and was later rechristened as the BCIM Forum. The final statement of that meeting was titled 'the Kunming Initiative', and it was by this name that the Forum was originally known, until political discretion suggested a more neutral denomination of the quadrilateral.[8] BCIM is a species of sub-regional cooperation, conceptually prioritising a sub-region of China (the province of Yunnan primarily, along with adjacent South Western provinces), a sub-region of India (particularly, India's North Eastern states and the Eastern state of West Bengal), along with the two intervening countries, Myanmar and Bangladesh.[9]

Initially, it was started as a four-nation conference convened jointly by institutions from the four countries, including the Yunnan Academy of Social Sciences from China, the Institute of Chinese Studies and the Centre for Policy Research from India, the Centre for Policy Dialogue from Bangladesh and cooperating institutions from Myanmar, and attended by scholars and academicians, representatives of Government, business and industry, as well as media-persons from all four countries.[10] In essence, it was initiated as a Track-II dialogue between these countries. The main purpose behind setting up such a grouping was to push for a combined endeavour by the four countries to increase connectivity, culture, trade and tourism ties and people-to-people contact amongst themselves and in the border regions in particular to address issues of trans-border crime like drug-trafficking, gun-running, illegal immigration etc. through increased inter-country cooperation and greater harmonisation of border policies.[11] Additionally, invoking the rhetoric of the 'Southern' or 'South Western' Silk Route, the BCIM aims to restore the historical arteries of overland connectivity that once linked India's Eastern seaboard and North Eastern states with China's South Western province of Yunnan through present-day Bangladesh and Northern Myanmar.[12]

So far, around a dozen meetings of the BCIM Forum have been conducted. The first meeting was held in Kunming in 1999, second in New

Delhi in 2000; then, after two years in 2002, the third meeting was held in Dhaka. The fourth meeting was held in Yangon in 2003, fifth in Kunming in 2004, followed by the sixth meeting in New Delhi in 2006, seventh in Dhaka in 2007 and eight in Nay Pyi Taw in 2009. The ninth BCIM Forum was held again in Kunming in 2011, and tenth in Kolkata in 2012. The last BCIM forum meeting was held in Cox's Bazar in December 2014.

One may note that the BCIM Forum made slow progress till 2013. It was only after the BCIM K2K Car Rally in 2013 that it began to pick up and the Governments of the four countries began to give due importance to BCIM. In March 2013, Chief Minister of West Bengal, Mamata Banerjee, flagged off the BCIM car rally. Around 80 participants from Bangladesh, China, India and Myanmar began their journey from Kolkata to reach Kunming via Jessore, Dhakha, Sylhet, Silchar, Imphal, Ka Lay, Ruili, Tengchong, Erhai Lake and Dali.[13] It can be seen that it was only in 2013, after the BCIM Car Rally, that BCIM got official recognition from the Chinese leadership as part of the Joint Statement issued at the end of the State Visit to India of the Chinese Premier, Li, in May 2013. He stated that:[14]

> The two sides [i.e. India and China] appreciated the progress made in promoting cooperation under the BCIM (Bangladesh, China, India, Myanmar) Regional Forum. Encouraged by the successful BCIM Car Rally of February 2013 between Kolkata and Kunming, the two sides agreed to consult other parties [i.e. Bangladesh and Myanmar] with a view to establishing a Joint Study Group on strengthening connectivity in the BCIM region for closer economic, trade, and people-to-people linkages, and to initiate the development of a BCIM Economic Corridor.

During Chinese Premier Li's India visit, India and China agreed to set up a joint working group to study the feasibility and implications of a BCIM-EC. So far, only two meeting have been held. The first meeting was convened in Kunming on December 19, 2013. The second was held in December 2014. Notably, the idea of establishing an economic corridor was initiated by India and China to run from Kolkata to Kunming, linking Mandalay and Dhaka. This will encompass an area of 1.65 million square kilometres and cover an estimated 4.4 billion people. As per the Joint working group, the plan would "advance multi-modal connectivity, harness the economic complementarities, promote investment and trade and facilitate people-to-people contacts".[15]

Importance of BCIM for Member Countries

Bangladesh

Bangladesh is the fourth poorest country in Asia, with a GDP of US$ 282.945 billion in Power Purchasing Parity (PPP) terms, after Afghanistan, Nepal and Myanmar. It is the eighth most populous nation in the world, with an area of just 147,570 sq km. It shares borders with just two countries—India and Myanmar. Its geographical location makes it dependent on India and, to a lesser extent, on Myanmar. Bangladesh is mainly an agrarian society. Although Bangladesh is rich in land and labour resources, it suffers from capital scarcity and BCIM could act as an amplifier in this regard.[16] In such a situation, in all likelihood, BCIM will prove to be the most beneficial for Bangladesh. Though Bangladesh is not a resource-rich country, it offers low cost manpower. By virtue of being surrounded by two resource-rich neighbours, Myanmar and India (NER), it is in a position to gain substantially. In addition to this, under the framework of BCIM, Bangladesh could act as a transit hub for many countries as many neighbouring countries like Nepal and Bhutan are land-locked.

China

China's main objective behind pushing for the BCIM-EC is to give a boost to its Southern-most landlocked Yunnan Province. Yunnan shares borders with Laos, Myanmar and Vietnam in the West and Thailand, Cambodia, Bangladesh and India in the South. From the 1990s, China has adopted a policy to open up its border provinces—particularly those which are landlocked—for cross-border economic cooperation. Encouraged by the success of its other sub-regional initiatives, particularly those with Southeast Asian countries, such as GMS, China strived to connect its Yunnan province with Southern neighbours. It may be noted that the Silk Road Economic Belt initiatives are also aimed at enabling connectivity in the sub-region, and contributing to regional connectivity.

BCIM forum is strategically important for China. Firstly, it gives China access to Myanmar's rich energy reserves—particularly after the opening up of Myanmar. Before coming out of Myanmar's self-imposed isolation, China was its major economic and strategic partner. Considering that Myanmar is gravitating towards the West and engaging other Asian countries, China is trying to find new ways to reach out to Myanmar through BCIM. Secondly, this sub-regional integration of economies will give China more confidence to showcase its economic ascendancy in the region. Thirdly, China shares no common border with Bangladesh, which is strategically very important to China. Reaching out to Bangladesh will give China unhindered access to the Bay of Bengal—and beyond.

India

There are several reasons why BCIM is vital to India. First, BCIM is a subset of India's Look East Policy objective. Hence, it holds immense importance in India's foreign policy manoeuvres. Second, the failure of SAARC drove India to found a regional organisation. The successful establishment of the BCIM fulfils India's need of playing a leadership in regional and sub-regional groupings.

Third, NER has been one of the less connected and underdeveloped zones of India. However, both the government and civil society are working actively to bring NER to the mainstream. Improving physical and digital connectivity is one of the principal focus areas in that regard.

As far as India and China are concerned, this is the only sub-regional grouping in which India and China are participating together. India-China bilateral trade stood at US$ 65 billion in 2013. However, the huge and consistent trade deficit still remains an irritant in India-China burgeoning trade relations. In 2013, trade imbalance touched US$ 31 billion in China's favour. The cooperation between India and China through BCIM-EC has the potential to reduce this trade deficit. It will also lead to a reduction in the cost of transportation between Kolkata and Yunnan.

Myanmar

Myanmar is now undergoing a transformation in its political, domestic, economic and social fabric. On the political front, Myanmar is moving from authoritative military governance to a more democratic system, while on the domestic front, the nominally-civilian U Thein Sein's Government is endeavouring to make peace with the ethnic groups, thereby ending a sixty-year internal conflict. Myanmar has also embarked on economic reforms which attempt to transform the economy into a market-oriented economy. Lastly, as the country steadily comes out of isolation, it is deviating from its earlier position on foreign relations. Instead of keeping itself restricted to a few countries, Myanmar has been endeavouring to engage with various countries of the world. In such a situation, when Myanmar needs to add credibility to its endeavours, sub-regional cooperation for this under-developed country is immensely important.

Although Myanmar wants to reduce its dependence on China, it wants to play safe. With the removal of economic and political sanctions by the US, Myanmar quickly moved to engage with the West, which led to a setback in Myanmar-China relations. However, Myanmar, whose reforms are still at a nascent stage, needs China for economic purposes, considering China is not only the largest trading partner of Myanmar but also the largest source of overseas investment in Myanmar.

Prospects

India and China are the biggest economies in Asia. Though they are still embroiled in half-a-century old boundary dispute, the possibility of engaging China through BCIM seems to be yielding constructive results on security and economic issues vis-a-vis India's North East. BCIM would provide India's North East an opportunity to showcase its geo-economic advantages besides strategic geo-political importance by way of establishing cross-border connectivity, and enhancing access to markets of neighbouring countries, making both production and marketing cost effective. So is the case with Yunnan. For both the countries, the issue of connectivity and establishing trade linkages with their peripheral regions are becoming areas of utmost importance. Once operationalised, BCIM-EC has the potential to address the issue of huge trade imbalances.

On the presence of India and China in the grouping, Professor Che Zhimin, then Deputy Director of the Economic and Technological Research Centre of the Yunnan Provincial People's Government), stated that if the two large developing countries, China and India, manage to cooperate in international affairs through such a mechanism, it will 'contribute to the establishing of the new multi-polar world order and [to] safeguard[ing] the peace and stability of Asia and the World.[17]

Implementation of the ideas of BCIM-EC will also prove to be beneficial to the economies of Bangladesh and Myanmar. Additionally, Myanmar's engagement with these three countries will give credibility to its reforms.

Pitfalls

Some fifteen years and around a dozen meetings on, the BCIM has not made substantial progress in realising the aim of the grouping in particular, and objectives of respective countries, in general. Far from spear-heading the process of opening up the continental route to East and Southeast Asia, it seemingly remains more or less as it was conceived, neither a 'bottom-up' nor a 'top-down' political/diplomatic engagement caught somewhere in limbo between 'Track-II' and 'Track-I', and destined, thereby, to practical inefficacy.[18] Although it is increasingly gaining prominence, the reluctance of the Governments of these countries to transform this Track-II sub-regional grouping into a Track-I sub-regional grouping is visible.

Second, volatility of border regions of all these countries is no hidden fact. For instance, India's Northeast is turning into a hub of insurgency. It is a home to as many as 30 armed insurgent groups. In the case of Myanmar, uncertainties regarding the country's political future linger until the 2015 General Elections are held. Cross-border cooperation with Bangladesh also comes with a risk. Operational economic corridor might lead to an increase in illegal migration from Bangladesh, hence affecting the tranquillity of border regions.

Third, there still exist problems between India and China. More than half-a-century old border dispute is an irritant in bilateral relations. On top of it, frequent border infiltration by the Chinese makes the issue all the more precarious. Though relations are not on a downward spiral, the border dispute nevertheless has the potential to derail relations to a significant level. One may argue that without addressing the border issue, BCIM-EC is not going to take meaningful shape, given that China is contesting claims on one of the North Eastern States—Arunachal Pradesh. Additionally, the huge trade imbalance in China's favour is proving to be a nightmare for India. Both countries require taking affirmative steps to solve the issue of trade imbalance before moving towards BCIM-EC.

Way Forward

Notably, it has been fifteen years and the sub-regional grouping is yet to take concrete shape. While progress has been slow, it should be kept in mind that this sub-regional arrangement has the potential to push for greater sub-regional integration. For India, the real challenge lies in realising sub-regional, regional and inter-regional connectivity with Bangladesh, Myanmar and countries of the Southeast Asian region. A well-networked NER is an essential precondition in that regard.

Given that the primary aim of BCIM is to give a boost to each country's borderlands, focus should be on enhancing people-to-people contact. It is logical that groupings like these take time to materialise; however, all the four countries need to step up cooperation so as to enhance sub-regional connectivity and push for the development of their respective border areas.

Six Conditions for a Successful BCIM-EC

In order to tap the fullest potential of the BCIM-EC, some steps need to be taken. It is in this context six conditions may be listed:

- **Mutual Investments:** More economic linkages are needed to ensure that India and China grow together and shed the baggage of mutual distrust. During his India visit in September 2014, Chinese President Xi Jinping promised around US$ 20 billion investments in India. It is important to convert such promises into reality.
- **More Joint Projects for Infrastructure Development:** India and China's initiatives to establish the BRICS bank (New Development Bank) and India's support for China-led Asian Infrastructure Investment Bank (AIIB) are two promising initiatives that have the potential to transform the underdeveloped patches, lying in the territories of the member countries into growth zones. AIIB can be of great help in developing infrastructure in Bangladesh, India and Myanmar.
- **India Should Seek Support From Japan, South Korea, Singapore and Australia:** India has to partner with major stakeholders of the Asia-Pacific in strengthening trade and investment inter-linkages, particularly with regard to developing its North East Region. BCIM-EC offers an unprecedented opportunity in engaging the major Asia-Pacific economies such as Japan, South Korea, Australia and Singapore, which are also the key countries in infrastructure development and power generation projects.
- **Equitable Outcomes:** An essential requisite for making BCIM-EC a success is active participation and share of Bangladesh and Myanmar as well. The grouping must not be limited to the perspectives of China and attempts must be made to ensure that this sub-regional grouping remains a mutually beneficial project for all.

- **More Communications:** Due to the lack of substantive people-to-people contacts, India-China relations have been mostly driven by their respective Central Governments. Unlike India's border with Myanmar, Bangladesh and even Pakistan, there are no ethnic communities (except Tibetans, which is a much complicated issue) along the two sides of the border that can effectively influence the relations. Therefore, there are no 'bottom up' pressures on the Government to bring more warmth into the border relations. More people-to-people contacts are needed to improve bilateral communications.
- **Resolving India-China Border Mistrust:**There needs to be mutually agreeable resolution of the boundary dispute, otherwise it would be extremely difficult for BCIM-EC to realise its fullest potential.

NOTES

1. Lindsey Powell. "In Defence of Multilateralism", *Global Environmental Governance: the Post-Johannesburg Agenda, (*New Haven: Yale Centre for Environmental Law and Policy, 2003), p. 3.
2. Robert O. Keohane. "Multilateralism: An Agenda for Research", *International Journal,* vol. 45, no. 4 (Autumn 1990), pp. 731-764.
3. John Ruggie. "Multilateralism: The Anatomy of an Institution", *International Organization,* vol. 46, no. 3 (Summer 1992), pp. 566-568.
4. Artatrana Gochhayat. "Regionalism and Sub-regionalism: A Theoretical Framework with Special Reference to India", *African Journal of Political Science and International Relations,* vol. 8, no. 1, (2001), p. 10.
5. Ibid.
6. Ibid.
7. Suisheng Zhao. "The Making of China's Periphery Policy", in Suisheng Zhao's (ed.), *Chinese Foreign Policy: Pragmatism and Strategic Behaviour,* (Armonk: East Gate Book, 2004), p. 256.
8. Patricia Oberoi. "The BCIM Forum: Retrospect and Prospect", (working paper, Institute of Chinese Studies Working Paper#1, 2012), p. 5.
9. Ibid., p. 14.
10. For more details, see http://www.icsin.org/BICM.aspx.
11. Ibid.
12. Oberoi, Patricia, op. cit, p. 2.
13. For more details, see, http://www.bcimcarrally.com/.
14. 'Joint Statement on the State Visit of Chinese Premier Li Keqiang to India, May 20, 2013', at http://www.mea.gov.in/bilateral-documents.htm?dtl/21723/Joint+Statement+on.
15. Ananth Krishnan, "BCIM Corridor Gets Push after First Official-Level Talks in China", *The Hindu,* December 12, 2013, http://www.thehindu.com/news/international/world/bcim-corridor-gets-push-after-first-officiallevel-talks-in-china/article5483848.ece.

16. M. Shahidul Islam. "China's Look South Policy and Bangladesh's Look East Policy: Convergences and Constraints" (Presented at a seminar on "China's Look South and Bangladesh's Look East Policy: Convergences and Constraints", organised by the Institute of Governance Studies of Brac University in The Daily Star Centre on 09 October 2013).
17. Che Zhimin quoted in Oberoi, Patricia. *op. cit,* p. 7.
18. Oberoi, Patricia. op. cit, p. 2.

9

BCIM-Economic Corridor: The Way Forward

Falguni Rajkumar

There is growing realisation that it is in India's interest to integrate its trade and commerce with its East Asian neighbours—including China—through transnational land connectivity through its NER. India has decided to simultaneously use this opportunity to improve the economic scenario in its NER. This approach of the Government of India (GoI) is certainly a welcome departure for the people of the NER in more ways than one. The LEP is seen as a fresh new initiative that gives tremendous hope to the neglected region.

This initiative is, however, bogged down primarily on the question of how satisfactorily India is able to address its external and internal security concerns in the region, which is surrounded by various countries. Part of the cause is the clear verdict in favour of growing sea trade between India and other Southeast Asian countries in comparison with the proposed continental land route. This inhibits most industrial and commercial enterprises from investing or committing themselves on the proposed land connectivity. Given these imperatives, especially when huge costs and investments are involved, the proposed BCIM-EC as well as the proposed land routes to Southeast Asia through the NER are bogged down or are, at the very least, progressing at an extremely slow pace.

This paper briefly analyses the BCIM-EC as part of the overall LEP of India, with specific reference to the NER, what it means to the people and the region as a whole, and explores reasons why and what needs to be done to actualise land connectivity in the interest of the NER and the country.

Introduction

India's ambitious LEP is understood differently at the national and regional levels. From the national perspective, it is unidirectional, meaning 'East' of Kolkata, while for the NER, the LEP is a multi-directional policy initiative. This is essentially because, unlike the rest of the country, the constituent states in the NER have international borders surrounded by four different countries in the North, East and South.

For the people of the NER, the LEP implies a major policy shift, both in the country's foreign as well as in its domestic policies. This is because the GoI and earlier, the British, had always considered and dealt with the NER essentially from the security point of view; thus, making the NER an integral part of the LEP in what is essentially an economic and commercially oriented policy decision is not only refreshing but is also seen as extremely significant. This 'shift'—by implication, 'reconciliation'—between the security and economic concerns in managing the NER, deflects criticism against the Central Government about the step motherly treatment meted out to the NER.

In spite of this, the GOI is not vigorously pursuing land connectivity through the NER since, descriptively, the land route primarily means road and rail connectivity that entails a greater people-to-people contact. Thus, even though the sea route may be good for commerce, true integration and 'contact' with the peoples of the region is best achieved through the land route. It is precisely this transformation in the nature of 'contact' amongst the people of the region in the future in a very sensitive region of Southeast Asia that inhibits GoI to aggressively pursue land connectivity to the 'East', especially through the Northern half of the NER. This is particularly so in the context of the sensitive troubled tri-junction of India, Myanmar and China through which the land corridor has to pass. In this situation, India has to carefully identify a route that meets both its geostrategic security needs on one hand, and the economic and commercial benefits on the other. The complexity of choice lies in fulfilling these two requirements.

Recontextualising LEP from the NER perspective:

There are some important factors that need to be elucidated in the context of the LEP in so far as the NER is concerned. First, the people of the NER consider the LEP—as also the BCIM and other similar policy initiatives—as a possible way for the region to overcome its present economic plight and underdevelopment. They are, therefore, highly sensitive to the use of terms like 'economic corridor' in defining the proposed land connectivity through the region, since the term gives an impression as if the NER is merely a 'corridor', a 'thorough-fare' through which goods and services will pass-without bringing any direct economic benefit to the region and to them. A better terminology, therefore, to define the BCIM route could be 'BCIM Regional Co-operation Corridor' (derived from Bangladesh-China-India-Myanmar Forum for Regional Cooperation), 'BCIM Industrial Corridor', instead of 'Economic corridor'. Second, the people living in the NER are 'border communities' whose lives will be greatly affected socio-culturally, environmentally and in many other respects—both positively as also adversely—as and when the region opens out to outsiders. Already, ethnically polarised and politically divided within due to several exogenous factors which have led to the fragmented underdevelopment of the states, the region will require necessary safeguards against any more intrusive divisive influences. Third, the LEP, from the NER perspective—including the BCIM—is a multi-directional policy initiative unlike the national perspective, which is unidirectional or singularly 'East' oriented. This difference arises because each of the constituent states of the NER which have different countries as their immediate neighbours demand different strategies and models for trade and commerce in conformity with their respective unique needs, levels of development, etc. Consequently, the LEP is sub-categorised into the various directional variants, based on the physical contiguity or proximity of these states with neighbouring countries.

The three sub-categorisations are (i) 'Look North Policy' (LNP) comprising Sikkim and Western Arunachal Pradesh with Bhutan, Eastern Nepal, the Autonomous Region of Tibet and China; (ii) 'Look South Policy' (LSP) involving the states of Meghalaya, Western Assam, Tripura and Mizoram, which directionally trade with Bangladesh; and (iii) 'Look East Policy' (LEP) involving the states of Arunachal Pradesh (Eastern Half), Nagaland, Manipur and Mizoram, which have propensity to trade with Myanmar. There is no 'Look West Policy' since the West for the NER is the rest of India, connected through the Siliguri Corridor—also known as the 'Chicken's Neck' in common parlance. Consequently, any form of transnational road connectivity through the NER must necessarily factor in, and recognise, these three directional orientations while pursuing either the Indo-ASEAN or the BCIM continental connectivity.

Why is BCIM important for the NER? The actualisation of the BCIM connectivity is important for the NER because (i) it will re-open road, rail and the all-important riverine transit routes to Kolkata through Bangladesh, thereby greatly reducing travel time between the NER and Kolkata. This also implies immediate access to the Bay of Bengal in the shortest possible time through Bangladesh; (ii) since the BCIM will be a multilateral agreement between Bangladesh, India, Myanmar and China, such an agreement will provide India, in the shortest possible time, a way out to obviate and overcome the hesitation that Bangladesh has of entering into a bilateral agreement with it for various reasons; (iii) in its historical perspective, the proposed BCIM connectivity through Bangladesh for India corrects a historical wrong by restoring the natural age-old connectivity that was discontinued at independence in 1947; and (iv) it is believed that since the BCIM has fewer participating countries, its implementation can be so much faster than the much larger Indo-ASEAN connectivity.

Seen from the NER perspective, the BCIM corridor has, even though only a Track II initiative, because of immediate benefits to the NER, is more critical and important than even the ASEAN land-route connectivity, which is a much bigger project requiring considerable investment and time to actually materialise.

Which route to Choose: It was pointed out at the outset that for India, any land or continental connectivity through its NER must meet the twin objectives of addressing its geostrategic security concerns and also fulfil its commercial and trade needs. Keeping these requirements in mind, India has three routes to choose for the BCIM—'economic corridor'—(i) the Asian Highway route, the Kolkata-Dacca-Silchar-Moreh-Tamu-Mandalay connectivity, (ii) the Stilwell (Ledo) route, which is the Kolkata-Dacca (Bangladesh)-Silchar-Shillong-Guwahati-Tinsukia-Ledo-Nampong (India)-Myitkyna (Myanmar)-Ruili Kunming (China) connectivity, (iii) to speedup projects like the Kaladan multimodal transport network through the southern tip of Mizoram or (iv) find any other Southern route that links the ASEAN countries avoiding the much-troubled tri-junction of North East India-Western Myanmar-South Western China region.

Of the three, the shortest route for the BCIM between Dacca and Kunming in China via Kolkata is the link through the Northern half of the NER, which has to pass through the troubled tri-junction where NER—Western Myanmar and South Western China region meet. This route is synonymous with the Stillwell Road. This route has several security related issues as compared to other routes in the region, and policy makers have, as such, felt it is best to avoid this portion of the Stilwell route.

The present thinking seems to veer around to the use of the Moreh-Tamu road, a part of the larger Indo-ASEAN trade corridor up to Mandalay, which is, in any case, already being upgraded and improved over the years by India. Then moving up North link to Ruili, at which point it joins the last stage of the Stilwell road as it enters China. This route is suggested since it traverses the southern half of the NER through the Moreh-Tamu sector to Mandalay, a part of the proposed Indo-ASEAN road connectivity, and avoids the troubled North western parts of the Sagaing Region and the Kachin State in Myanmar altogether.

This BCIM route will, therefore, link Dhaka (formerly known as Dacca) to Mandalay via Western Assam-Moreh (India)-Tamu (Myanmar), as part of the Asian Highway in the first stage (through Kalemyo) on the 'Friendship Road' that India has financed and built for the Myanmar Government, before touching Mandalay. In the next stage from Mandalay, it will move North East towards Lashio and Muse in North East Myanmar and enter Ruili (China). In the third stage, using the last phase of the Stilwell Road, it will lead to Dali and Chuxiong (China), before ending in Kunming.

This route, a combination of the Asian Highway routes, the India-Myanmar-Thailand Trilateral Highway (IMTTH) and the Stilwell Road in parts, will not only be cost effective but, importantly, address India's security concerns by avoiding the highly sensitive part of Arunachal Pradesh altogether, and also the troubled North-West Sagaing and Kachin region of Myanmar. The proposed route is the one followed by the K2K motor-rally held recently in the beginning of 2013. It traverses through roads most of which are reasonably good condition to start with. A few patches, however, need to be taken up for up-gradation immediately—while the rest can be addressed in a progressive manner over time.

Enhance bilateral engagements with Bangladesh and Myanmar: As part of the BCIM, as also of Indo-ASEAN trade relations, India should expand its bilateral engagements with Bangladesh and Myanmar, its two immediate neighbours, on priority irrespective of the time taken to actualise the BCIM or ASEAN connectivity. These two countries are historically—and now commercially—important for the people of the NER, especially as the same ethnic groups and communities live on either side of the international border. These divisions, which took place in different times of history, not only divided families but also disrupted the natural flow of people, trade and commerce between neighbours. The irony, however, is that both these 'divisions' of people into politically defined spaces did not eradicate the emotional ties and connections, nor did it stop the commerce and exchange of goods and commodities all along the newly demarcated international borders. If one analyses the various problems of the NER, one discovers that this is one of the major irritants.

In the context of the BCIM or the Indo-ASEAN connectivity, this aspect needs to be elaborated as a point in case to highlight why there is an urgent need for implementing mutually beneficial trade and business relationship between India, Bangladesh, Myanmar and China for the NER of India.

If one examines the sub-categorised 'Look South Policy' (LSP) of the NER, which involves the states of Meghalaya, Western and South-Western Assam, Tripura and Western half of Mizoram, one will find that essentially, it is based and structured on the descriptions of the once-flourishing trade and commerce between the predominantly upland tribal communities of these states with the people and communities of the Great Plains of Bangladesh, before the partition of the sub-continent in 1947. It emerges that the inter-dependence of people living on both sides of the international boundaries on each other is compelled by the very topography and circumstances of their living conditions in these areas, and for which they have no alternative. In short, people living in these areas have no choice but to depend on each other for survival.

Similarly, the LEP, from the NER perspective which involves the states, Nagaland, Manipur, the Eastern parts of Arunachal Pradesh and Mizoram, directly trade with people living in the entire length of the Western borders of Myanmar. The same factors that compel trade and commerce between the people of the NER living in the border areas and Bangladesh also compel those people living the border areas between the NER and Myanmar.

Consequently, since 1994, the Border Trade Agreement between India and Myanmar, even though restrictive, has been beneficial. The new FTA with ASEAN, of which both India and Myanmar are signatories, will remove further restrictive tariff barriers, thus greatly benefiting both countries. Besides, for the people in these states abutting Myanmar, who share anthropological, socio-cultural affinities and ties, establishing people-to-people contact through trade would greatly help in resolving many potential irritants and problems in these border areas for Governments.

It is important to understand that Myanmar is the only member country of the BCIM forum or the ASEAN with a both common land and maritime border with India through the NER. It is in this sense also that Myanmar is the most important country for the success of any of the Asian trans-continental route, as it alone can provide access to nations in these transnational ventures. In short, the success of both these multilateral partnerships depends greatly on how Myanmar responds.

Both Myanmar and Bangladesh, because of their physical proximity, are—both legally and mostly illegally—major sources of goods and items that the people of NER need. This is primarily because, currently, the entire NER depends on the rest of the country for all essential commodities through a long, torturous and unsatisfactory supply-chain. This supply-chain most often breaks down for various reasons, both man-made and natural. Due to non-availability/shortages/inadequate quality of essential commodities in these border areas, most communities and people living in these areas and towns depend even today on supplies made available to them through sources from Bangladesh and Myanmar through border trade, legally or illegally. Moreover, as the quality and type of the food items, grains, etc from these two neighbouring countries are much more suited to the NER palate, people of the NER prefer these items than those supplied from other parts of India at much higher costs. Since these are most often clandestinely and illegally brought in from across the borders, it adds to the headache of an already overburdened law enforcement system, and adds another dimension to the law and order issues of the area.

If, therefore, either the BCIM or ASEAN road connectivity is implemented, most items required in the NER can be instead made available from Myanmar at much cheaper rates. In addition, the NER will get another source of essential commodities the region requires regularly. This arrangement can be mutually beneficial to both countries by not only enhancing bilateral trade and commercial activities, but as observed, also ensuring an alternative source of supply the NER requires.

Enhance people-to-people contact: Perhaps one of the most important aspects in which maximum impact can be made by BCIM connectivity is in enhancing people-to-people contacts between the four participating countries, especially in education, health, tourism and cultural exchanges. As an example of how such people-to-people contact helps in fostering a better relationship with India's neighbours is the case when on December 24, 2013, a team of doctors and experts from Shija Eye Care Foundation of Shija Hospitals and Research Institute (SHRI), Imphal (Manipur) went to Myanmar to conduct 200 free cataract surgeries at Monywa General Hospital at Monywa Township in Myanmar's Sagaing division. The team was led by Dr Kh Palin as part of the hospital's Mission Myanmar Phase II. The Mission is a state-sponsored collaborative effort of the Governments of Manipur and Myanmar, Indian Consulate General and Shija Eye Care Foundation. Special permit has been granted to the team for the Mission by the Government of Sagaing Division. It is estimated that there are over 1.8 million Myanmar nationals who are suffering from cataract, and there is lack of health care facilities in Myanmar.

This Mission was made possible because it was a follow-up after the visit of H.E. U That Aye, Chief Minister of Sagaing Division of Myanmar and HE U Ye Mynt, Chief Minister of Mandalay, along with other delegates to the Shija Hospitals and Research Institute, Langol (Imphal) on November 21, 2013. The dignitaries participated in the celebration of Manipur Sangai Festival along with 165 Myanmarese, who had travelled from Myanmar to witness the Manipur Sangai festival. For the first time, the visit of the dignitaries and the large delegation from Myanmar, who flew in by a Golden Myanmar Airlines flight, heralded the landing of an international flight in Imphal, as reported by the local press in Manipur. It was during this visit that the two Chief Ministers from Myanmar invited the doctors from the Shija Hospitals and Research Institute, for a second Mission to Myanmar. The first Mission Myanmar had already taken place in May 2013, in which 103 free cleft lip and palate surgeries were performed successfully on 87 patients. The objective of the Second Mission Myanmar was also to enhance the relationship between the two nations.

Similarly, such initiatives can be taken up in the field of education. For instance, the Rajiv Gandhi Indian Institute of Management, Shillong, runs a one year Post Graduate management course for Indian executives in collaboration with the College of Management, Ocean University of China, located in Qingdao, wherein Indian executives spend almost six months in China and the rest in Shillong in India. Similarly, various areas for enhancing people-to-people contact in tourism can be explored.

Preparing the NER: There are some areas of concern that need to be addressed before implementing BCIM connectivity in the NER. First and foremost is the lack of basic infrastructure like roads, power, communication, market, digital connectivity etc, which are far below national averages and are in bad shape in the region. In this connection, it is necessary to complete all approved road works being undertaken by the Ministry of Surface Transport in the NER under its flagship programme, the National Highway Development Programme (NHDP), particularly the Special Accelerated Road Development Programme for the North East (SARDP-NE). Part of the SARDP-NE roads, which form part of the proposed ASEAN and BCIM route, should get outmost attention to ensure that these are completed well in time.

Secondly, the people of NER are highly vulnerable 'border communities' and, as the region opens up, their lives are bound to be affected in many respects, socio-culturally as also the physical environment. It is, therefore, necessary that people in the region are psychologically prepared to accept these changes, including the presence of 'outsiders' in their midst. Already, ethnically polarised and politically divided within, which has led to the fragmented underdevelopment of the region and states, the region will require necessary safeguards against exogenous divisive influences which may be exerted on them by the presence of large numbers of foreigners.

Such observations are being made since already some ethnic groups and communities in the region are demanding the introduction of the 'Inner Line Permit' system, which prohibit the free entry of 'outsiders' into their states. The NER, with its unique and mixed tapestry of ethnicities, communities, diverse tribal and nontribal sub groups, needs to prepare its population to face impending changes in their lives.

NER as one single economic entity - need for introspection: One of the most exasperating experiences in the NER for any potential investor is the divided polity, a legacy of state formation based on ethnic identities. This has not only led to the political polarisation of the NER, but has also led to fragmented development due to break-down in planning in the region. The prevalent condition leads to considerable hurdles for investors in getting projects and plans approved, since they are compelled to obtain a number of approvals and permissions from different states. Given the fact that the economic environment around the NER's international borders is fast changing, and where neighbouring countries and their governments are extending and providing support, incentives and opportunities to invest, Indian entrepreneurs prefer to locate their projects in adjoining countries rather than in the NER. This situation of having many small states—even though politically desirable—creates its own problems for investors, inhibiting them from investing in the region. There is a need for these states to work together as a single group to enthuse industrialists and entrepreneurs to invest.

Logically, this realisation should lead leaders of the region—political and economic—to redefine their relationship with each other. Even though at first glance this may appear to be a shift from state-centralism to regionalism, the reorientation actually shows that the adjustment is actually a move from unbridled chaotic development to one of inter-dependence and planned growth based on cooperation and partnership. It will be a process and approach which will give rich dividends to each state in the long-run, especially when the states are expected to take on the challenges posed by the LEP in the near future. The Central Government should try to encourage and help these states to evolve a mechanism by which they can jointly face new challenges in the coming days.

Need for LEP Coordination office for the NER: To ensure that the BCIM and Indo-ASEAN continental road connectivity are appropriately addressed, it is necessary to immediately set up the BCIM (as also the Indo-ASEAN) regional coordination office in the NER to take all necessary steps.

The following steps are suggested: (a) Put in place a common-authority for planning, execution and coordination amongst the various agencies and departments of the GoI and the participating State Governments to set up an India-ASEAN Centre in New Delhi, (b) have a branch office of this common-authority in the NER. This common authority must coordinate and monitor the various functionary institutions and organisations, both state agencies and private investors, which can be modelled on the lines of the GMS office. This agency or setup (by whatever name it may be called) in New Delhi should be tasked to plan ahead and draw-up action plans for effective interagency coordination and functioning of various agencies involved and also oversee projects linked to the LEP in the NER. For the regional office, the GoI should entrust this work to the NEC with representatives from the Ministry of External Affairs (MEA) and the Ministry of Commerce.

In fact, when this author was the Secretary of the NEC, with Mr Manishanker Aiyer as the Minister for DoNER and Chairman of NEC, the process of setting up of such an office in the NEC Secretariat was started. Two officers, one from the MEA and another from the Ministry of Commerce, were to function under the control of the Secretary, NEC, in Shillong. The MEA had appointed and posted the Regional Passport Officer at Guwahati to function as the MEA's representative in the NEC. Orders from the Ministry of Commerce were also expected. This proposal needs to be vigorously pursued if the LEP in the NER has to see the light of day.

Concluding Observations

Given the fact that GoI continues to consider the NER as a high security risk and vulnerable region, the proposed unhindered and unencumbered movement of people into and through the region following the opening of the NER inhibits Governments from taking too much liberty in changing the ground rules. It is no wonder, therefore, that attempts at implementing the BCIM continental connectivity through the NER, especially in the Northern half of the NER, remains half-hearted and a far cry from what progress could have been achieved. For the NER, this lack lustre progress has several implications, direct and indirect, as it affects them in more ways than one, and especially because it takes away the hope of a better and prosperous future. Keeping this in mind, this paper has suggested a compromise route that will effectively take care of India's security concerns and also ensure the unencumbered movement of goods and services through the NER for the region's development, for both the BCIM forum and also the Indo-ASEAN trade connectivity.

It must, however, be mentioned that success and putting in place any regional and sub-regional project like the BCIM and Indo-ASEAN continental connectivity is also contingent on fulfilling several conditions. It not only involves mobilisation and availability of adequate resources to finance the project to begin with, but also implies the prevalence of good-will and understanding amongst participating countries. Quite often than not, these international efforts mean compromises, sacrifices and adjustments that can impinge on sensitive issues of national interest of participating countries. In short, all these effectively means overcoming various political, economic and socio-cultural issues by meaningfully adjusting and meeting the distinct and varied administrative institutionalised practices that different countries follow. Given this narrative, successful implementation and actualisation of the BCIM economic corridor will largely, therefore, depend on how diligently participating countries perform their respective roles and are able to adjust with one another.

ICWA Report on BCIM-EC

Seminar on BCIM Economic Corridor (BCIM-EC)

Indian Council of World Affairs

December 5, 2013

Indian Council of World Affairs hosted a one-day brainstorming seminar on Bangladesh, China, India and Myanmar-Economic Corridor (BCIM-EC) on December 5, 2013. Academicians, journalists and diplomats from the NER and New Delhi participated in the deliberations. The discussion focussed on issues of trade, connectivity and tourism as well as cooperation in social cultural and academic fields, and gave several recommendations to the MEA on their deliberations on BCIM-EC. Following are the salient points and suggestions made during discussions.

Session I: Enhancing Regional Connectivity: Role of BCIM-EC

- India is open to idea of BCIM.
- An improved India-China relationship is an opportunity to expand cooperation along the BCIM-EC.
- Trade and cooperation in power generation and distribution could be one option for enhancing connectivity and spur economic growth in the region. Three models could be adopted in this regard: (a) bilateral trade in electricity, such as between Bangladesh and India, India and Myanmar, and India and China, (b) Pool-based exchanges by creating power grids of sub-regional countries exchanging/trading electricity, and (c) Wheeling facility i.e. centralise and re-distribute it.
- NER should not only be used for transit in BCIM-EC but opportunities such as investment and trade hubs should be created in the region so that it ushers progress and prosperity in the region.

- Kolkata and Guwahati should also be connected with BCIM-EC (K2K).
- It will be useful to explore prospects of direct air connectivity to support BCIM-EC.

Session II: Trade and Investment Potential of BCIM-EC

- Trade between BCIM countries has been buoyant, but there are still many avenues which need to be explored. Regional and Central Governments should take efforts to tap this potential.
- India's Line of Credit extended to Bangladesh and Myanmar is doing well, but the disbursement of credit process should be expedited.
- Illegal/informal trade has been taking place across borders, and this should be regularised by creating more Customs points and additional border trade points.
- Sub-regional groupings such as GMS, BIMSTEC and BCIM should also be integrated where possible, to enhance the effectiveness of BCIM-EC. They should coordinate their activities rather than compete.

Session III: BCIM-EC: North East Perspective

- Development of peripheries has always been a challenge for large nations, including India and China. However, GMS, Greater TUMEN Initiative and IMT-GT can be considered as models of economic growth. Both India and China could cooperate in BCIM to develop their underdeveloped peripheries.
- There is a need to develop economic infrastructure of NER before operationalising BCIM, otherwise Kunming—which is economically developed—will become the core and NER will remain a periphery.
- There is a need to operationalise land trade and, for greater integration of the region, various routes should be considered simultaneously.

Session IV: Panel Discussion on BCIM-EC: The Road ahead

- The nomenclature of the BCIM-EC could be BCIM Growth Zone (BCIM-GZ). In its present form, it gives the impression that the

EC facilitates trucks and freights on highway, and NER does not gain anything. Therefore, it would be better to rename it as BCIM-GZ.

- BCIM-EC should not be limited to trade but also include people-to-people cooperation in education, health and tourism amongst BCIM countries.
- There are concerns that development and extraction/exploitation of resources in the NER will have an impact on the environment. Special attention should be given for preservation of ecology and wildlife preservation, and the BCIM-EC developed in a sustainable manner.